The Bush Theatre in association with Live Theatre, Newcastle
present the world premiere of

Chalet Lines

by Lee Mattinson

6 April – 5 May 2012
Bush Theatre

12 – 29 September 2012
Live Theatre, Newcastle

This production is generously sponsored by
Gianni & Michael Alen-Buckley

Chalet Lines

by Lee Mattinson

Cast

Jolene	**Robyn Addison**
Paula/Sylvia	**Sian Breckin**
Loretta/Edith	**Monica Dolan**
Abigail	**Laura Elphinstone**
Barbara	**Gillian Hanna**

Creative Team

Director	**Madani Younis**
Associate Director	**Omar Elerian**
Designer	**Leslie Travers**
Lighting Designer	**Tim Mascall**
Sound Designer	**Tom Gibbons**
Dramaturg	**Ché Walker**
Casting Director	**Chloe Emmerson**
Dialect Coach	**Daniele Lydon**
Company Stage Manager (on the book)	**Nick Hayman**
Assistant Stage Manager	**Lizzie Donaghty**
Production Assistant	**Robert K Harm**
Costume Supervisor	**Amy Cook**
Head of Stage	**Dave Blakemore**
Scenic Artist	**Bethany Ann MacDonald**
Make-up Artist	**Victoria Stride**
Set Construction by	**Factory Settings**

The Bush would like to give thanks to: Wendy Barnfather, Gez Casey, Max Roberts and the team at Live Theatre, West London Centre for Sexual Health, English Touring Theatre, Central School of Speech and Drama, MProductions, Morrisons, Donmar Warehouse,Tony Donaghy, Alexandra Isaacs, Sarah Barnes, Nichollas Humphrey, Hereford Cider Museum, Paul Roughton at Stage Electrics, The Home Brew Shop, Xcatalogue Hillingdon, Sian Thomas, Annie Orwin, Daniele Lydon, Anna Bolton, Tracy Whitwell, Jaqueline King, Dorothy Atkinson, Rebbeca Staton, Victoria Bewick, Max Perryment

Robyn Addison Jolene

Theatre includes: *Mongrel Island, Realism* (Soho); *The Rivals* (Theatre Royal Bath/West End).

Television includes: *More Than Words, Starlings, Survivors, Waterloo Road, George Gently, Casualty, The Street, Dalziel and Pascoe.*

Robyn was nominated as an *Evening Standard* Outstanding Newcomer in 2011 for *Mongrel Island* and *The Rivals.*

Sian Breckin Paula/Sylvia

Theatre includes: *The Baron* (Old Vic & Time Warner Ignite); *The 24 Hour Plays* (Old Vic); *Christine* (New End).

Television includes: *Scott & Bailey, DCI Banks: Aftermath, George Gently, Casualty, Heartbeat, The Royal.*

Film includes: *Tyrannosaur, Donkey Punch.*

Short film includes: *Alice* (directed by Marianne Elliot); *Shift* (directed by Mike Figgis).

Monica Dolan Loretta/Edith

Theatre includes: *Birth of a Nation, The Glory of Living* (Royal Court); *She Stoops to Conquer, A Laughing Matter* (National Theatre/Out of Joint); *King Lear, The Seagull, The Taming of the Shrew, A Midsummer Night's Dream, Henry V, Coriolanus, Measure for Measure, Unfinished Business* (RSC); *Macbeth* (Out of Joint); *Sliding With Suzanne* (Royal Court/Out of Joint); *Jane Eyre* (Shared Experience/West End); *Hayfever* (West End); *The Walls* (National Theatre); *The Glass Menagerie* (Royal Lyceum).

Television includes: *Appropriate Adult, U B Dead, Excluded, Occupation, The History of Mr Polly, Poirot, The Commander, Wallis and Edward, Tipping the Velvet, Judge John Deed, The Gift.*

Film includes: *Sightseers, The Arbor, Never Let Me Go, Within the Whirlwind, King Lear, Topsy-Turvy, A Midsummer Night's Dream.*

Laura Elphinstone Abigail

Theatre includes: *Top Girls* (Chichester Festival Theatre/Trafalgar Studios); *A Month in the Country* (Chichester Festival Theatre); *Marine Parade* (Brighton Festival); *Pains of Youth, Women of Troy* (National Theatre); *Bedroom Farce* (West Yorkshire Playhouse); *Far From the Madding Crowd* (ETT); *Glass Eels* (Hampstead); *Tom and Viv* (Almeida); *Pictures of Clay* (Manchester Royal Exchange); *Crucible* (RSC/West End) *Heartbreak House* (Watford Palace Theatre); *Scenes from an Execution* (Hackney Empire); *Breathing Corpses, Country Music* (Royal Court).

Television includes: *Doctors, My So Called Life Sentence, Tess of the D'Urbervilles*.

Film includes: *The History Boys*.

Gillian Hanna Barbara

Recent theatre includes: *Brighton* (Garter Lane Theatre, Waterford/tour); *Beauty Queen of Leenane* (Theatre Royal Waterford/tour); *Many Roads to Paradise* (Finborough); *Ivanov* (National Theatre); *Night Songs, Fireface* (Royal Court); *Medea* (Queen's).

Television includes: *Strike Back, George Gently, The Kindness of Strangers, Poirot, Brookside*. She is also the voice of Auntie Swift in the children's series *Mist: The Story of a Sheepdog Puppy*.

Film includes: *Oliver Twist, The Heart of Me, Mr Nice, All the Queen's Men, Les Misérables*.

Gillian was a founder member of the feminist theatre company The Monstrous Regiment. She also translates plays from French and Italian, including *Accidental Death of an Anarchist* and *Elizabeth: Almost by Chance a Woman* (Dario Fo), *A Woman Alone* (one-woman plays by Franca Rame and Dario Fo), and *Le Renard du Nord* by Noelle Renaude (all published by Methuen). She is currently working on *Arse up in a Ditch* by Fausto Paravidini.

Amy Jane Cook Costume Supervisor

Theatre designs include: *65 Miles, Once Upon a Time in Wigan* (Hull Truck/Paines Plough); *Hamlet* (Young Vic/Maria Theatre); *Sixty-Six Books, Flooded Grave, Where's my Seat?* (Bush); *The Water Engine* (Old Vic Tunnels); *The Pride* (BeMe Theatre, Munich); *The 8th* (Paines Plough); *A Midsummer Night's Dream* (Broadway Theatre); *W11* (Gate); *She Stoops To Conquer* (Hoxton Hall); *It's About Time* (Nabokov/ Latitude); *Love's Labour's Lost* (Guildford Castle); *Limehouse Nights* (Limehouse Town Hall); *Ignite* (Complicité/Artsdepot); *Manor* (Soho/Tristan Bates).

Film includes: art direction on *Fred's Meat* (North London Film Awards).

Amy has also worked as an event/installation designer for the Bush Theatre, the Nabokov Arts Club, Polka Theatre and at Standon Calling Festival. Amy is the associate designer with Kandinsky Theatre Company and the resident designer with Theatre 6. She trained at Motley Theatre Design School.

Omar Elerian Associate Director

Omar is Associate Director of the Bush Theatre.

His latest directing credits include the acclaimed site-specific production *The Mill – City of Dreams* (Bradford, Yorkshire); *You're Not Like The Other Girls Chrissy* (The Stage Best Solo Performance Award winner, Pleasance Attic, Edinburgh); *Testa di Rame* (Teatro Fortezza Vecchia, Italy); *Les P'tites Grandes Choses* (Maison de Arts du Cirque et du Clown, France) and *L'Envers du Décor* (Théâtre Les Enfants Terribles, France). He was also Associate Director on Jericho House's *The Tempest* (part of the Barbican's BITE '11 season in St Giles Cripplegate).

Tom Gibbons Sound Designer

Recent designs include: *Island* (National Theatre/tour); *Romeo and Juliet* (Headlong/tour); *Disco Pigs* (Young Vic); *Dead Heavy Fantastic* (Liverpool Everyman); *Plenty* (Crucible Studio, Sheffield); *Encourage The Others* (Almeida); *Love Love Love* (Royal Court/tour); *Wasted* (Paines Plough/tour); *The Knowledge, Little Platoons, 50 Ways To Leave Your Lover, 50 Ways To Leave Your Lover@Xmas* (Bush); *Shivered, Faith, Hope and Charity, The Hostage, Toad* (Southwark Playhouse); *Sold* (Theatre503); *The Chairs* (Ustinov, Bath); *The Country, The Road To Mecca, The Roman Bath, 1936, The Shawl* (Arcola); *Bagpuss, Everything Must Go, Soho Streets* (Soho); *The Machine Gunners* (Polka); *Holes* (New Wimbledon Studio); *Terror Tales* (Hampstead Studio); *Faustus* (Watford Palace/tour); *Faithless Bitches* (Courtyard); *FAT* (Ovalhouse/tour); *Just Me Bell* (Graeae/tour); *Fanta Orange, Blue Heaven* (Finborough); *Pitching In* (Latitude Festival); *US Love Bites* (Old Red Lion/Tristan Bates); *Pendulum* (Jermyn Street).

Associate designs include: *The Aliens, Broken Space Season* (Bush).

Tom trained at Central School of Speech and Drama and is resident sound designer for the international physical theatre company Parrot{in the}Tank.

Tim Mascall Lighting Designer

Theatre includes: *The Importance of Being Earnest* (Regent's Park Open Air Theatre); *Well* (Apollo); *The Vagina Monologues* (Wyndhams); *Potted Potter, An Evening of Wonder* (Garrick); *Ruby Wax: Losing It* (Duchess); *Why The Whales Came* (Comedy); *Derren Brown: Enigma* (Adelphi); *Something Wicked This Way Comes* (Old Vic); *The Lady Of Burma* (Riverside Studios); *Professor Bernhardi, Rose Bernd, The Roman Bath, Jenufa* (Arcola); *How To Disappear Completely and Never Be Found* (Southwark Playhouse); *Breakfast With Jonny Wilkinson* (Menier Chocolate Factory); *Marilyn and Ella* (Theatre Royal Stratford East); *Bloody Poetry* (Jermyn Street); *Hundreds and Thousands* (Soho); *Cotton Wool* (Theatre503).

Regional UK work includes: designs for Oxford Stage Company, Mercury Theatre Colchester, Derby Theatre, New Wolsey Ipswich and Sherman Theatre, Cymru. Touring productions include: *Bad Jazz* and *Gizmo Love* (ATC); *Teenage Kicks, Stones in His Pockets* and *Trainspotting* (MGL); *Pete and Dud: Come Again* and *The Alchemist* (Seabright Productions).

Dance includes: *Latin Fever* (RGL at Peacock Theatre/tour); *Into the Hoods* (Peacock); *Entangled* (The Place).

Opera includes: *The Gamblers* (Royal Festival Hall); *Atalanta* (RCM/ Britten Theatre); *Mahagonny Songspiel, Das Wunder Teatre* (Poliziano Theatre, Montipulciano).

Musicals include: *My Fair Lady* (Kuala Lumpur); *Bells Are Ringing* (Union); Trevor Nunn's production of *A Little Night Music* (Central Theatre, Budapest).

Lee Mattinson Writer

Theatre includes: *No Wire Hangers* (Soho); *Donna Disco* (Chicken Pox Fox/Live Theatre); *Me & Cilla, M&S S&M, Orlando Spoon, Julian Scary, I Heart Morrissey, Liquorice, Funny Valentine, Shitty Shitty Bang Bang, 6C Nativity, Circus Girl* (Live Theatre); *Jonathan Likes This* (National Theatre/Live Theatre); *The Bang Gang* (Bad Fox Theatre Company); *Rabbit Rabbit Rabbit* (Northumberland Theatre Company); *Chocolate* (West Yorkshire Playhouse); *Paper Men Hold Hands* (Monster Productions); *Swan Song* (New Writing North/Live Theatre); *Blue and Grey, Panda* (People's Theatre); *Freddy Hearts Freddie, Me Fatty* (Ugly Sister Productions); *The Window Letters* (Theatre in the Mill).

His most recent play, *Crocodiles*, was shortlisted for The Verity Bargate Award 2011.

Television includes: *Scallywagga*.

Film includes: *Harvest*.

Radio includes: *Me & Cilla* ('The Wire' Radio 3), *Prom, Snowglobe* (Radio Newcastle).

He recently completed his first novel, *Orlando*.

Leslie Travers Designer

Recent designs include: *Cinderella* (New National Theatre, Tokyo); *Tannhäuser* (Estonian National Opera); *Guilio Cesare* (Opera North/Teatro Nacional de São Carlos, Lisbon); *The Merry Widow*, *I Capuleti e i Montecchi*, *The Children's Crusade* (Luminato Festival, Toronto; winner of Dora Mavor Moore Award Best Opera Production 2010, nominated for best overall design in all catagories); *Jenufa*, *Les Contes d'Hoffmann*, *L'arbore di Diana*, *Palau de les Artes* (Valencia); *Twelfth Night* (Chichester Festival Theatre); *The Duchess of Malfi* (West Yorkshire Playhouse).

Leslie has also worked as a long-term collaborator with Madani Younis; designs include: *Streets of Rage*, *Caravan*, *Silent Cry* (West Yorkshire Playhouse).

Leslie trained in theatre design at the Wimbledon School of Art.

Ché Walker Dramaturg

Writing includes: *Been So Long* (Royal Court); *Fleshwound* (Royal Court: winner, George Devine Award, Arts Council Award Most Promising Writer); *Crazy Love* (Paines Plough/Òran Mór); *The Frontline* (Shakespeare's Globe); *Been So Long: The Musical* (Young Vic/ETT); *Lovesong* (Pleasance Dome/ETT).

Directing includes: *Been So Long: The Musical* (Young Vic/ETT); *Lovesong* (Pleasance Dome/ETT); *Fog*, *Blue Surge*, *Etta Jenks* and *Achidi J's Final Hours* (Finborough); *Danny And The Deep Blue Sea* (Southwark Playhouse); *Estate Walls*, *Little Baby Jesus* (Ovalhouse/ETT); *Balm In Gilead*, *Mouthful Of Birds* (Rada).

Che is an Associate Artist at the Bush.

Madani Younis Director

Madani is Artistic Director at the Bush. He was the Artistic Director of Freedom Studios in Bradford, Yorkshire. His most recent work for the company was the site-specific work, *The Mill – City of Dreams*. He has also worked nationally and internationally as theatre director, writer and practitioner.

Appointed in 2002 as the Director of Red Ladder Theatre Company's Asian Theatre School, Madani staged seven productions for the company: *Streets of Rage* (2002); *Silent Cry* (regional and national tour. 2003–2004); *Freeworld* (an international collaboration with the Studio Theatre Damascus, Syria, 2004); *Caravan* (West Yorkshire Playhouse, 2005); *Freefalling* (Red Ladder Theatre Company, national tour, 2005); *A Waiting Room for Journeying Souls* (Peepul Centre, Leicester, 2005), and *Doors* (Red Ladder Theatre Company, national tour, 2007).

He originally trained in film, and his debut short film *Ellabellapumpanella*, commissioned by the UK Film Council, was screened at the Cannes Film Festival in May 2007.

He was the recipient of the Decibel Award at the South Bank Awards show in 2006.

About the Bush

The Bush Theatre is a world-famous home for new plays and an internationally renowned champion of playwrights and artists. Since its inception in 1972, the Bush has pursued its singular vision of discovery, risk and entertainment from a distinctive corner of West London. Now located in a recently renovated library building on the Uxbridge Road in the heart of Shepherds Bush, the theatre houses a 144-seat auditorium, rehearsal rooms and a lively café bar.

www.bushtheatre.co.uk

bushgreen

bushgreen is a social-networking website for people in theatre to connect, collaborate and publish plays in innovative ways. Our mission is to connect playwrights with theatre practitioners and plays with producers, to promote best practice and inspire the creation of exciting new theatre.

bushgreen allows members to:

- Submit plays directly to the Bush for our team to read and consider for production

- Connect with other writers, directors, producers and theatres

- Publish scripts online so more people can access your work

- Read scripts from hundreds of new playwrights

There are thousands of members and hundreds of plays on the site.

To join, log on to **www.bushgreen.org**

At the Bush Theatre

Artistic Director	**Madani Younis**
Executive Director	**Angela Bond**
Associate Director	**Omar Elerian**
General Manager	**Eleanor Lang**
Assistant Producer	**Sade Banks**
Theatre Manager	**Annette Butler**
Marketing Manager	**Sophie Coke-Steel**
Theatre Administrator	**Cat Gray**
Technical Manager	**Neil Hobbs**
Development Officer	**Lucy Howe**
Production Manager	**Anthony Newton**
Associate Producer	**Carolina Ortega**
Producer	**Rachel Tyson**
Associateships, Internships and Attachments	
Commercial Consultant	Nathalie Bristow
Development	Lottie Wake
Marketing Assistant	Simone Finney
Bushgreen Administrator	Karis Halsall
Deputy Production Manager	Jessica Harwood
Leverhulme Trust Associate Playwright	Sabrina Mahfouz
Press Representative	Kate Morley
Box Office Supervisor	Gareth Walker
Duty Managers	Gemma Bergomi, Simone Finney, Michael McBride, Chloe Stephens, Gareth Walker, Matt Watson,
Front of House Assistants	Benedict Adeyemi, Devante Anglin, Hannah Barter, Lily Beck, Gemma Bergomi, Jules Morgan Bert, Nick Blakeley, Nathan Bryon, Simone Finney, Lucy Foster-Perkins, Aaron Gordon, Sophie Howard, Amy Hydes, Michael McBride, Laura McCullagh, Natalia Moozarmi, Hannah Smith, Chloe Stephens, Roland Szabo, Matt Watson
Duty Technicians	Carly Hook, William Lewis, David Mooney, Simon Perkins

* **Bold** indicates full-time staff; regular indicates part-time/temporary.

The Bush Theatre, 7 Uxbridge Road, London, W12 8LJ
Box Office: 020 8743 5050 Administration: 020 8743 3584
email: info@bushtheatre.co.uk
The Alternative Theatre Company Ltd (The Bush Theatre) is a registered charity and a
company limited by guarantee. Registered in England No. 1221968. Charity No. 270080

Be there at the beginning

The Bush Theatre would like to extend a very special 'Thank You' to the following patrons, corporate supporters and trusts & foundations whose valuable contributions continue to help us nurture, develop and present some of the brightest new literary stars and theatre artists.

Lone Star
Gianni Alen-Buckley
Michael Alen-Buckley
Francois & Julie Buclez
Siri & Rob Cope
Jonathan Ford
  & Susannah Herbert
Catherine Johnson
Caryn Mandabach
Miles Morland
Lady Susie Sainsbury
James & Virginia Turnbull
Nicholas & Francesca Whyatt

Handful of Stars
Anonymous
Micaela & Chris Boas
Jim Broadbent
Clyde Cooper
Blake & Michael Daffey
David & Alexandra Emmerson
Catherine Faulks
Chris & Sofia Fenichell
Christopher Hampton
Douglas Kennedy
Mark & Sophie Lewisohn
Adrian & Antonia Lloyd
Mounzer & Beatriz Nasr
Georgia Oetker
Claudia Rossler
Naomi Russell
Charles & Emma Sanderson
Eva Sanchez-Ampudia
  & Cyrille Walter
Joana & Henrik Schliemann
Jon & NoraLee Sedmak
Larus Shields
John & Amelia Winter

Rising Stars
Anonymous
Nick Balfour
Tessa Bamford
David Bernstein & Sophie Caruth
Simon Berry
John Bottrill
David Brooks
Karen Brost
Maggie Burrows
Clive Butler
Matthew Byam Shaw
Benedetta Cassinelli
Tim & Andrea Clark
Claude & Susie Cochin de Billy
Angela Cole
Matthew Cushen
Irene Danilovich
Michael & Marianne de Giorgio
Yvonna Demczynska

Judy Cummins & Karen Doherty
Ruth East
Charles Emmerson
Jane & David Fletcher
Lady Antonia Fraser
Vivien Goodwin
Sarah Griffin
Hugh & Sarah Grootenhuis
Mr & Mrs Jan Gustafsson
Martin & Melanie Hall
Sarah Hall
Hugo & Julia Heath
Roy Hillyard
Urs & Alice Hodler
Bea Hollond
Zaza Jabre
Simon Johnson
Ann & Ravi Joseph
Davina & Malcolm Judelson
Paul & Cathy Kafka
Rupert Jolley & Aine Kelly
Kristen Kennish
Tarek & Diala Khlat
Heather Killen
Sue Knox
Neil LaBute
Eugenie White
  & Andrew Loewenthal
Isabella Macpherson
Peter & Bettina Mallinson
Charlie & Polly McAndrew
Michael McCoy
Judith Mellor
Roger Miall
David & Anita Miles
Caro Millington
Pedro & Carole Neuhaus
Kate Pakenham
Mark & Anne Paterson
Julian & Amanda Platt
Lila Preston
Radfin Courier Service
Kirsty Raper
Clare Rich
Sarah Richards
Joanna Richards
Robert Rooney
Damian Rourke
Karen Scofield & LUCZA
Russ Shaw & Lesley Hill
Saleem & Alexandra Siddiqi
Melanie Slimmon
Brian Smith
Sebastian & Rebecca Speight
Nick Starr
Andrew & Emma Sutcliffe
The Uncertainty Principle
The van Tulleken family
Francois & Arelle von Hurter

Hilary Vyse & Mark Ellis
Trish Wadley
Amanda Waggott
Dame Harriet Walter
Edward Wild
Peter Wilson-Smith & Kat Callo
Alison Winter
Jessica Zambeletti

Corporate Supporters
Spotlight
John Lewis, Park Royal

Lightbulb
The Agency
AKA
Mozzo Coffee & La Marzocco
Talk Talk Ltd

The Bush would also like to thank **Markson Pianos**, **Westfield** and **West 12 Shopping & Leisure Centre**

Trusts and Foundations
The Andrew Lloyd Webber
  Foundation
The Daisy Trust
The D'Oyly Carte Charitable
  Trust
EC&O Venues Charitable Trust
The Elizabeth & Gordon Bloor
  Charitable Foundation
Foundation for Sport and the
  Arts
Garfield Weston Foundation
Garrick Charitable Trust
The Gatsby Charitable
  Foundation
The Goldsmiths' Company
The Grocers' Charity
The Harold Hyam Wingate
  Foundation
Jerwood Charitable Foundation
The John Thaw Foundation
The Laurie & Gillian Marsh
  Charitable Trust
The Leverhulme Trust
The Martin Bowley Charitable
  Trust
The Hon M J Samuel Charitable
  Trust
The Thistle Trust
Sir Siegmund Warburg's
  Voluntary Settlemen

World Stages London

World Stories for a World City
A season of theatre
May 2012

10% multi-buy discount
worldstageslondon.org.uk
Booking & Enquiries –– 0844 412 4314

CHINA

WILD SWANS
Young Vic
13 April – 13 May

EUROPE

THREE KINGDOMS
Lyric Hammersmith
03 May – 19 May

THE WORLD

BABEL
Caledonian Park, Islington
08 May – 20 May

MIDDLE EAST

THE BELOVED
Bush Theatre
21 May – 09 June

SOUTH AFRICA

THE SUIT
Young Vic
21 May – 16 June

INDIA

WAH! WAH! GIRLS
– A British Bollywood Musical
Sadler's Wells Peacock Theatre
24 May – 23 June

Supported by

About Live Theatre

From its base on Newcastle's quayside, Live Theatre produces work as varied and diverse as the audiences it engages with. To do this it:

- Creates and performs new plays of world-class quality

- Finds and develops creative talent

- Unlocks the potential of young people through theatre

Founded in 1973, the theatre was recently transformed via a £5.5 million redevelopment. The result is a beautifully restored and refurbished complex of five Grade II listed buildings with state-of-the-art facilities in a unique historical setting, including a cabaret-style theatre, a studio theatre, renovated rehearsal rooms, a series of dedicated writers' rooms as well as a thriving café, bar and pub.

www.live.org.uk

At Live Theatre

Chief Executive	**Jim Beirne**
Artistic Director	**Max Roberts**
Operations Director	**Wendy Barnfather**
Administrator – Directors	Clare Overton
Literary Manager	**Gez Casey**
Literary Officer	Rosie Kellagher
Administrator – Literary Department	Degna Stone
Production Manager	**Drummond Orr**
Technical Manager	**Dave Flynn**
Senior Technician	**Mark Tolan**
Finance Officer	Catherine Moody
Marketing Manager	**Claire Cockroft**
Marketing & Press Officer	**Emma Hall**
Marketing & Press Officer	Amy Corbett
Marketing & Press Assistant	**Melanie Rashbrooke**
Development Manager	Gillian Firth
Associate Director, Education & Participation	**Paul James**
Drama Worker	**Amy Golding**
Drama Worker	Phil Hoffmann
Administrator – Education & Participation	**Sam Bell**
House Manager	**Carole Wears**
Deputy House Manager	Michael Davies
Duty Manager	Holly Sykes
Duty Manager	Ben Young
Administrator – Events & Hires	**Nicole Huddart**
Stage Management & Duty Technicians	Paul Aziz, Heather Robertson, Tom Saunders
Frontline Staff	Mark Gerrens, Emily Wray, Rosa Aers, Ben Young, Holly Skyes, Helen Tuffnell, Caroline Liversidge, Amy Berry, Katie Dent, Matthew Greenhough, Emily Merrit, Matty Poppl, Nina Berry, Sian Thorpe, Chris Foley, Nina Scott, Charlotte Wainwright, Camille Burridge

* **Bold** indicates full-time staff; regular indicates part-time/temporary.

CHALET LINES

Lee Mattinson

To the Chien (Victoria), with love

Characters

BARBARA, *the nana*
LORETTA, *the mother*
JOLENE, *the daughter*
ABIGAIL, *the daughter*
PAULA, *the hen*
EDITH, *the great-nana*
SYLVIA, *the bridesmaid*

This can be achieved with five actors with the following doubling:

Actor One	Barbara
Actor Two	Loretta, Edith
Actor Three	Jolene
Actor Four	Abigail
Actor Five	Sylvia, Paula

The play is set over fifty years in the same chalet at Butlins, Skegness.

This text went to press before the end of rehearsals and so may differ slightly from the play as performed.

Scene One

2010.

Thursday 22nd July. BARBARA*'s seventieth birthday.*

Lights up on a Butlins' chalet.

The chalet door and a bathroom door lead off. There are two single beds, a sofa bed, small bedside table, dressing table with mirror, wardrobe.

ABIGAIL, *thirty, is downstage centre with a pack of Juicy Fruit chewing gum.*

At the dressing table, she unwraps single sticks of Juicy Fruit, lays them out along its edge to resemble piano keys.

She stretches her fingers, plays her 'piano', closes her eyes, quietly sings a verse of 'Don't Let the Sun Go Down on Me' by Elton John.

ABIGAIL *stops, opens the top drawer of the dresser, sweeps her Juicy Fruit piano out of sight in one swift and nifty movement, as:*

JOLENE, *twenty-eight, enters, with a bin bag full of inflated birthday balloons, texting into her phone, as:*

JOLENE. Is 'bell end' hyphenated?

ABIGAIL. I don't think so.

JOLENE. I'll just put all one word.

   Beat.

ABIGAIL. Are they on their way?

JOLENE. Who?

ABIGAIL. Mam and Nana.

JOLENE. Dunno.

ABIGAIL. Why don't ya say 'penis'?

JOLENE. I'm tryin' to give him the horn, not a GSCE Science.

ABIGAIL. 'Male gland'?

JOLENE. Who died and made you Pam Ayres? I'm puttin' 'bell end', he can like it or lump it –

There. Kiss. Send.

ABIGAIL. Is he comin' tonight?

JOLENE. That's what I've said.

ABIGAIL. What?

JOLENE. That the plans've been well and truly scuppered.

ABIGAIL. He'll be gutted.

JOLENE. I've give it a sexy edge so's he'll not think I'm just bein' frigid.

ABIGAIL. Right.

JOLENE. He'd promised to take uz trampolinin' afters, to cement the engagement, and I want him to know I'm still well up for that.

ABIGAIL. Ya scared of heights –

JOLENE. Aye, but look at my tits, these tits were made for trampolinin'.

ABIGAIL. Do ya think Nana's alright?

JOLENE. She's fuckin' livid, Mam'll never live this down.

ABIGAIL. Did ya hear her trump?

JOLENE. No.

ABIGAIL. When she accused the manager of bein' a Nazi, she did a sneaky trump, I heard her.

JOLENE. She maybes did it intentionally, as a little fanfare to illuminate her point?

Beat.

ABIGAIL. Do ya think Paula'll come?

JOLENE. Doubt it, it's been way too long.

Where did you slink off to?

ABIGAIL. I couldn't bear everyone lookin' when she started throwin' pineapples, I hate raised voices.

JOLENE. I love it but, after about ten minutes, Nana's voice just started soundin' like a guinea pig.

ABIGAIL. Shoutin' makes uz feel physically sick.

JOLENE. They'll be there all night, demandin' a refund on a meal they've not even had.

ABIGAIL. I wasn't that hungry anyway.

Beat.

Jolene?

JOLENE. What?

A text-message alert.

ABIGAIL. What's he said?

JOLENE. LOL and four kisses.

ABIGAIL. Brilliant.

JOLENE *hitches up her bra.*

JOLENE. Oh, aye, it's the trampolines for me tonight –

Enter LORETTA, *forty-eight – carrying several Tesco bags of banners, party poppers, decorations – and* BARBARA, *seventy, carrying a cake box.*

What happened?

BARBARA. What didn't happen.

LORETTA. Turns out they'd cancelled our reservation cos we failed to give ample notice we might be a bit late –

BARBARA. You failed to give ample notice we might be a bit late.

LORETTA. I didn't think it'd be that big an issue.

BARBARA. I dunno why we bothered bookin'?

LORETTA. It was me that bothered bookin', I've had the chalet booked since Christmas, I booked that when I booked this –

BARBARA. Overusin' the word 'book's not gonna magic up a later bookin', is it?

ABIGAIL. It was only about ten minutes.

BARBARA. I complained till I was blue in the face, Jolene –

JOLENE. We heard –

BARBARA. Twelve year old if he was a day –

LORETTA. Not a hint of sympathy, had he, Mam?

BARBARA. Not a modicum of understandin' of what it is to mark an occasion –

JOLENE. He was ninety-nine per cent acne –

BARBARA. There's ya savin' grace right there, if he cannet wash his face I doubt he washes his hands.

Paula would've put him in his place –

LORETTA. Do ya wanna cava, Mam?

BARBARA. She'd've handcuffed herself to a pot-wash and refused to move –

LORETTA. Is that a yes?

BARBARA. Yes.

LORETTA. Lasses?

JOLENE. I think I need a one.

ABIGAIL. No, thank you.

LORETTA *opens a bottle of cava, proceeds to pour drinks over the next section, hands them out.*

BARBARA. Where'd you pair get to?

ABIGAIL. We thought it best to meet ya back here.

BARBARA. Embarrassed, were ya, me at my age firin' at all cylinders?

JOLENE. Ya were an absolute scream.

BARBARA. Did I swear?

LORETTA. At one point, ya called him a 'backwards wanker'.

BARBARA. He shouldn't've been so vague with his protocol, his policy, his colour-coded seatin' plan, he can stick them up his arse.

JOLENE. I bet ya told him that, too –

BARBARA. I've a good mind to march over to Billy Butlin himself, give him what for.

ABIGAIL. I think he's dead.

BARBARA. If he's not, he'll wish he was once I've tore a strip off him.

Has Paula called?

LORETTA *ignores her, tops up her drink.*

Ya'll have to let her know we'll not be there, she'll be devastated.

LORETTA. I'll text her –

BARBARA. Don't text her, ring her, she might not see a text.

JOLENE. What we gonna do?

BARBARA. Get this, Jolene, tell her, Loretta, the mockery they're makin' of us.

LORETTA. They've agreed to ship a table over, bring the individual courses to the door.

BARBARA. Meals on bastard wheels, I ask ya.

JOLENE. Well, that's alright.

BARBARA. It makes *Come Dine with Me* look like positively Michelin-starred.

LORETTA. I've a good mind to send them my phone bill, if I rang that Kaleidoscope once a week to organise tonight, I phoned them twenty times.

BARBARA. It'll be down to that Polish lass ya kept gettin'.

LORETTA. Polish or Russian, I couldn't decipher.

BARBARA. Ya should've asked to be put on to someone northern.

ABIGAIL. I'm sure it was an honest mistake.

BARBARA. Aye, ya mother's mistake, the jury's still out on whether it was honest or not.

JOLENE. Will I ask Christopher if there's anythin' he can do?

BARBARA. It's too late now for any fuss, far too late.

I will just say that I was so very lookin' forward to tonight.

LORETTA. Don't be like that –

BARBARA. I'd've loved to have been surrounded by balloons and my loved ones in that restaurant tonight, a machine gun of party poppers explodin' around uz, a standin' ovation from the other holidaymakers, the compliments of a chef, but, oh, no –

LORETTA. Ya'll only upset yaself.

BARBARA. If I could afford the coffin, I'd be better off dead.

LORETTA. There's balloons there, we can throw somethin' together, make do –

BARBARA. Woop-de-fuckin'-do.

LORETTA. I've gone to far too much trouble for tonight to end in disaster, I've a vision as glorious as yours.

BARBARA. It was spellbindin' in my head, Loretta.

LORETTA. It's still spellbindin' in mine.

Beat.

BARBARA. I was so excited to see our Paula.

JOLENE. She'll come, Nana –

LORETTA. We'll just have to do it in here –

BARBARA. Granted, it's not as shitty as it used to be, but it's hardly the Kaleidoscope.

JOLENE. No, but if they're bringin' a table over we can make it nice for ya.

BARBARA. Ya cannet polish a turd, Jolene.

LORETTA. We don't have to polish it, we just have to thumbtack a balloon to the end of it.

Well?

BARBARA. Phone our Paula, see what she says.

Silence.

Anyone?

LORETTA. It doesn't matter what she says.

BARBARA. Just ascertain she's comin', that she's en route and we'll decide from there, there's no point to nowt if she's not comin' –

LORETTA. Of course she's comin' –

BARBARA. Well, go on then.

LORETTA. There's no reception in here.

JOLENE. Ya get four bars in the bathroom, if ya sit in the sink.

BARBARA. Needs must, Loretta, howay.

Exit LORETTA *to the bathroom, closes the door.*

ABIGAIL. Have you got Paula's number, Nana?

BARBARA. I'm useless with mobiles.

ABIGAIL. Right.

BARBARA. I've got ya mam's old one, it's like cartin' round a shoebox.

JOLENE. It's a proper olden-day one, isn't it?

BARBARA. To be fair, I only use it for Texty Bingo.

JOLENE. Texty Bingo?

BARBARA. Bingo via text, ya not heard?

JOLENE. How much?

BARBARA. A pound a number.

ABIGAIL. Do ya ever win?

BARBARA. No, but it's just nice to receive a text, isn't it, to know there's someone thinkin' about uz.

ABIGAIL. I'll text ya.

BARBARA. Ya know what they do, though, and I dunno how the hell they do it but when ya get an eleven, a legs eleven, ya phone whistles when ya open the message, it does a 'whit-woo'.

JOLENE. How do they do that?

BARBARA. I dunno but that alone's worth the quid –

BARBARA *wolf whistles a 'whit-woo'*.

Enter LORETTA.

Where is she?

LORETTA. Sittin' in traffic and cursin' like a banshee.

BARBARA. Hates bein' late and always has.

ABIGAIL. Brilliant.

LORETTA. She said to hang fire, have a glass of cava, since ya seventy and deserve it –

BARBARA. That I deserve it, she said that?

LORETTA. Aye, and that a nice family meal in here sounds like the perfect plan –

BARBARA. A nice family meal, did ya hear that, Jolene?

JOLENE. Aye.

ABIGAIL. That sounds lovely.

BARBARA. That does sound lovely, Loretta, how long again?

LORETTA. Not long, she assured uz.

BARBARA. She'll bloody make tonight, will our Paula.

JOLENE. What will I do about my Christopher?

LORETTA. He can just come here.

JOLENE. If ya sure that's alright, Nana? Although I should point out it is a family occasion and he is, technically, practically, family.

BARBARA. The more the merrier.

JOLENE. When's this table comin' then, cos I'll have to text him, let him know?

LORETTA. 'Soon as', they said.

JOLENE. I'll tell him 'soon as'.

Over the next section, JOLENE *texts, sends.*

ABIGAIL. We could always make it out later for a drink?

BARBARA. We'll see what our Paula fancies when the bairn arrives.

LORETTA. If we get in anywhere for a drink.

ABIGAIL. It's The Camp Champ's Championship tonight.

BARBARA. Right.

ABIGAIL. The budget holiday answer to *Opportunity Knocks.*

BARBARA. I've been before.

ABIGAIL. Was it a marvel?

BARBARA. What's that thing with the Scotch lass with the eyebrows?

ABIGAIL. I dunno.

BARBARA. Dressed in a chintzy pillowcase, nowt to look at till she opened her mouth.

JOLENE. Susan Boyle?

BARBARA. Aye, Susan Boyle, well, it wasn't as good as the thing she didn't win but I did enjoy it all the same.

LORETTA. What?

BARBARA. Whatever it is our Abigail's bangin' on about.

ABIGAIL. The Camp Champ's Championship –

LORETTA. She's not deaf.

ABIGAIL. Only, I thought, if we could head there, I could do ya a tune on a piano for ya birthday.

LORETTA. It's probably not your cup of tea, Mam.

ABIGAIL. One of ya favourites from when ya were little, 'White Cliffs of Dover' or somethin'?

BARBARA. I'm not that bloody old.

ABIGAIL. Or one that I've chose for ya myself?

BARBARA. I don't want any fuss.

ABIGAIL. It's no fuss, I've been practisin' –

LORETTA. Well, she said 'no', Abigail, let her have her day.

Ya know, the more I think about it, it might be nicer in here for the meal –

BARBARA. We're hardly puttin' the Royal Weddin' to shame.

JOLENE. I can paint ya nails, if ya like?

BARBARA. Oh, aye, I wanna look trendy for our Paula.

JOLENE. Howay then –

BARBARA. I don't want them neon again.

JOLENE. Neon went out with the Ark, Nana.

BARBARA. Get you, Jeff Banks.

Over the next section, JOLENE *proceeds to paint*
BARBARA*'s nails.*

LORETTA. Will I put balloons all the way round the top of the
room or just spot them about suggestively?

JOLENE. All the way, Mam.

BARBARA. Ya've enough of them, ya'd think I was seven not
seventy.

LORETTA. It was as much for fifty as it was for twenty.

BARBARA. How long did it take ya to blow them up, if ya
don't mind uz askin'?

LORETTA. Claude did them, bless him, he had to have a blast
of his inhaler twice.

JOLENE. One went off in his face, didn't it, Mam?

LORETTA. He fuckin' shit himself.

JOLENE. I wouldn't use thumbtacks, Mam, they'll have the
paint off.

BARBARA. They'll have the walls off the plight of them, if ya
wanna use anythin', ya wanna use Blu-Tack –

LORETTA. I know what I'm doin'.

JOLENE. At least they've painted it.

BARBARA. A lick of paint does not a chalet make.

JOLENE. It's all the rage, Nana, they call it shabby chic.

BARBARA. And I call it shabby shit.

How is your Claude?

LORETTA. Joined the gym.

BARBARA. What's brought that on?

LORETTA. You tell me.

BARBARA. Ya'd think they'd not let him with his asthma.

JOLENE. He goes most days after work, doesn't he, Mam, badminton, spinnin', that sort of metrosexual shit.

LORETTA. So he says.

BARBARA. Ya wanna join him, Loretta.

LORETTA. I'm as metrosexual as the next man, Mam, that's twice now we've been to Zumba, isn't it, Jolene?

JOLENE. Twice.

BARBARA. Do you not fancy it, Abigail?

ABIGAIL. I'm not really one for dancin'.

LORETTA. She wouldn't even do hokey-cokey at her own weddin'.

JOLENE *puts the finishing touches to* BARBARA*'s nails.*

BARBARA. That me done, is it?

JOLENE. They alright?

BARBARA. What a gorgeous-coloured nail lacquer, what do they call that?

JOLENE. Ginger Ninja.

ABIGAIL. They really suit ya.

BARBARA. I'd love another cava, me.

LORETTA. Ya gonna be mortal.

BARBARA. Not till our Paula gets here –

LORETTA. Jolene?

BARBARA. That's reason enough to celebrate.

JOLENE. Top uz up.

Over the next section, LORETTA *pours more drinks, dishes them out.*

BARBARA. Workin', then, is it?

LORETTA. What?

BARBARA. Claude, is he built like a brick shit-house now?

LORETTA. I couldn't tell ya the last time I saw him with his top off.

JOLENE. If anythin', me and Christopher are the opposite, I struggle to keep his clothes on, well, I say I struggle, I should but I don't.

LORETTA. There'll come a day there's nowt to undress for, believe you me.

JOLENE. No, we're gonna be full-throttle honeymoon for ever, I've told him, I want breakfast in bed till the day I die and not just crumpets, I want full English, the works.

Over the next section, LORETTA *unpacks the decorations.*

BARBARA. Every day was Valentine's for ya late granddad, even before the Alzheimer's.

LORETTA. Umpteen times I reminded him about my birthday. I know there's folk that don't bother, that let it go by, but –

ABIGAIL. Last week?

LORETTA. Last week. Your Charlie popped round, did he not say?

ABIGAIL. He didn't say.

LORETTA. Just a couple of quiet drinks on the patio, only a handful of people, no sign of Claude, or you, but magic all the same.

ABIGAIL. Ya didn't ring –

LORETTA. He's always some excuse when it comes to me.

BARBARA. Marriages are like yo-yos, Loretta, me and ya dad were the same.

JOLENE. I've all this to look forward to.

BARBARA. He once refused to hug uz for six years.

LORETTA *pulls out a banner. It's twisted, she attempts to unknot it, as:*

Do ya still kiss with tongues?

LORETTA. We've not had time, what with him workin' all hours –

BARBARA. The mortgage'll not pay itself.

LORETTA *becomes frustrated, pulls at it, almost breaks it.*

LORETTA. I dunno what he's thinkin' half the time –

BARBARA. The last place you wanna go's inside a man's mind –

LORETTA. I know what he's not thinkin' –

BARBARA. It'll be all sheds and porn –

LORETTA *suddenly stops.*

LORETTA. He's not thinkin' about me.

BARBARA. Do ya not wanna give Paula another try?

LORETTA. I'm nippin' over that seven-eleven for Blu-Tack –

ABIGAIL. I'm sorry about ya birthday, Mam, I've been that busy I didn't think –

LORETTA. Busy doin' what? Nowt as per?

BARBARA. I'm just ever so slightly concerned she might've had a car crash or, worst case, ran out of petrol.

LORETTA. Can I just finish this?

BARBARA. Get her rang and tell her we need an ETA, we wanna be ready for her.

LORETTA. Right.

BARBARA. And do it in here where I can hear –

LORETTA. Fine.

LORETTA *takes out her mobile, finds the number, rings.*

BARBARA. Is it ringin'?

LORETTA. Aye.

BARBARA. Whatever she says, as soon as she says it, repeat it back to uz, word for word –

LORETTA. She'll be drivin' –

BARBARA. She'll not want to pick up to that attitude if she's not.

LORETTA. It's still ringin' –

BARBARA. Smile, it makes ya sound happier –

LORETTA. It's gone to voicemail.

BARBARA. Pass it here, I'll leave her a message –

BARBARA *tries to grab the phone,* LORETTA*'s having none of it.*

LORETTA. No –

BARBARA. I wanna do it –

LORETTA. Leave off, Mam –

(*Into phone.*) Hi, Paula, it's just Loretta, we're just wonderin' where ya are and whatnot, how long ya gonna be, that sort of shite.

Give uz a buzz back when ya can, we're just sittin' waitin' on the table, we've not ordered yet but I imagine we will be soon enough, so, ya might wanna get a shake on, lots of love.

BARBARA (*shouts*). See ya soon, darlin' –

LORETTA *ends the call.*

Drivin', no doubt, a very careful driver is our Paula.

LORETTA. I'm worried about that cake sweatin' itself to mush.

JOLENE. Ya should've asked them to keep it there and bring it back over.

BARBARA. She'll be here, though, I know she will.

(*To* JOLENE.) Did ya hear back off your Christopher?

JOLENE. No, but that just more than likely means he's had to stay on.

BARBARA. Work them hard, do they?

JOLENE. They're essentially singin' and dancin' slaves.

BARBARA. It used to be quite a reputable thing to be a redcoat, I heard Princess Anne started out as a one.

Have you met him, Abigail?

ABIGAIL. I've seen the picture on her phone.

JOLENE. Did I show you the picture on my phone, Nana?

BARBARA. We've all seen it.

LORETTA. On the hour, every hour.

JOLENE. I can't wait for ya to meet him, he's immense. And so clean, he takes all his clothes off to have a shit.

BARBARA. What a gentleman.

JOLENE. He's my full stop at the end of God knows how many years of heartache.

BARBARA. It's no less than ya deserve.

Have ya picked ya bridesmaids?

JOLENE. I've had them on standby my whole life. Abigail'll be maid of honour, obviously, and I'll make sure Christopher takes Charlie on his stag night, I want them to be the best of friends –

LORETTA. Ya should've brought him this weekend.

ABIGAIL. Who?

LORETTA. Shouldn't she, Mam, have brought Charlie?

BARBARA. Oh, aye, he's a bonny lad is your Charlie.

ABIGAIL. He's workin'.

LORETTA. He's not, he's off till Tuesday now – (*To* BARBARA.) he's on a new rota, four on four off, it's a much better fit for him.

BARBARA. And such a wonderful eye for decor, that's a bloody show home you live in –

ABIGAIL. It was me that decorated it –

LORETTA. Ya only picked the colours, he put in the labour.

ABIGAIL. Them cushion covers were knitted from scratch –

LORETTA. Ya can tell.

JOLENE. Do ya think I should learn how to knit, what with uz bein' an up-and-comin' housewife?

BARBARA. Ya know what I really love about your Charlie, though?

ABIGAIL. What?

BARBARA. He can do a flat-pack.

LORETTA. And hold a decent conversation while he does, three quarters of an hour last week we talked about the Great Wall of China –

BARBARA. When was it I was round last?

ABIGAIL. I can't remember.

BARBARA. I'd took our Abigail that *Take a Break* with Carol Vorderman's struggle with cystitis smeared up the front and there he was, Black & Decker rotary drill in hand, constructin' a IKEA BILLY bookcase –

LORETTA. He put some shelves up in my box room to allow uz to catalogue my back catalogue of *Bella*.

BARBARA. Had a Daffy Duck T-shirt on but it hid nowt. (*To* ABIGAIL.) If I'd've known how to navigate ya central heatin', I'd've whacked it up to full in the hope that his trousers'd go transparent too –

ABIGAIL. Nana –

BARBARA. I'll make no bones about it, love, you live in paradise.

ABIGAIL. I live in no such place.

LORETTA. He's hilarious, too, isn't he, Mam?

ABIGAIL. He only puts it on for you.

BARBARA. He has me in kinks.

ABIGAIL. He's dull as dishwater.

LORETTA. You are.

Beat.

JOLENE. I just hope ya love him as much as I do.

LORETTA. Who?

JOLENE. Christopher, Mam.

LORETTA. He had me at 'strippin' for a shit'.

JOLENE. Cos I know it's been whirlwind and that there's folk that say ya can't hurry love, let alone marriage, but it's up to me this, it's women's intuition, cos ya just know, don't ya, Nana?

BARBARA. Course ya do and how long's it been now?

JOLENE. Today's day two.

LORETTA. Ya like a modern-day Craig David with tits.

JOLENE. I almost crapped my slacks when he proposed to uz over that buffet lunch –

LORETTA. Ya've said.

JOLENE. He didn't buy uz a ring cos he thought I might've said no, but he's point-blank promised to purchase uz a one at the weekend. I said I wanted topaz what with it –

LORETTA. Bein' ya birthstone, we know –

BARBARA. Eee, our little Jolene, married. I never thought I'd see the day anyone'd want to spend the rest of their lives with you.

JOLENE. It's like a film, isn't it?

ABIGAIL. Which one?

JOLENE. *Titanic*, probably. (*To* ABIGAIL.) We'll be able to do the marriage equivalent of double datin', won't we?

ABIGAIL. Yeah.

JOLENE. Waitin' for our lads to go to the toilet and then comparin' notes, what works, what doesn't work, workin' out what solutions we can fathom –

ABIGAIL. Me and Charlie don't really go out –

JOLENE. I read in *Cosmo* that the first six months of any relationship is all about 'settin' and maintainin' sexual and domestic boundaries.'

ABIGAIL. We've been married twelve year –

JOLENE. And what works?

ABIGAIL. 'What works'?

JOLENE. What's ya secret?

LORETTA. If it's Charlie ya wanna know about, ask me, he's round most nights for his tea.

JOLENE. What for?

LORETTA. Let's just say when the spark went, the spaghetti bolognese wasn't far behind –

ABIGAIL. Stop feedin' him and he'll stop comin' –

LORETTA. I like feedin' him.

Beat.

JOLENE. Re: the weddin' dress, I know exactly the one I want.

BARBARA. Can ya not just wear mine like Abigail?

JOLENE. The one I like's from this dead posh shop.

BARBARA. There's nowt so posh as an heirloom.

LORETTA. I bet it's stratospheric with your keen eye for fashion.

JOLENE. Basically, it's white.

LORETTA. It sounds gorgeous.

JOLENE. With lines of crystal radiatin' out from my tits so I look like a big bright star shinin' in the sky on a night –

BARBARA. Denise Welch wore a very similar one to last year's TV Quick Awards.

JOLENE. Do ya think Redcoat Christopher'll get married in his red coat?

BARBARA. They tend to, don't they, like the armed forces.

JOLENE. I don't care what he's in, as long as he's stood next to uz.

LORETTA. You'll be such a blushin' bride.

JOLENE. I will, won't I?

Cos, I know I've had more shags than Fred West, but it's not about sex, is it, it never is, it's about love. And I've finally found, after lookin' high and low, I've located that love.

And I know ya've heard it all before, with Jason and Darren and Kieran and even Liam from the Esso garage, but Christopher's the one, isn't he, this is my big chance.

BARBARA. Ya've kissed enough frogs.

JOLENE. I've told him, I said, I want a three-bedroom semi within the first six months, two holidays a year, not to Butlins, obviously, somewhere nice, abroad, like Greece or somewhere, babies, a dishwasher, umpteen dogs, that array of top-notch stuff –

LORETTA. Alright –

JOLENE. I've a scrapbook detailin' the whole thing, if anyone wants to see?

LORETTA (*snaps*). We've all seen it, Jolene.

JOLENE. Alright.

LORETTA. All I'm sayin' is take it down a level –

JOLENE. I'm up a height here –

LORETTA. I'm not havin' a go, I'm just sayin' don't spontaneously combust about it.

JOLENE. I bet you were the same –

BARBARA. The rate ya mam went through diaries, Anne Frank wants to be ashamed she ever picked up a fountain pen –

JOLENE. I just wanna get it right.

LORETTA. And ya will, but marriage is bloody hard work –

JOLENE. I know that –

LORETTA. It's about holdin' ya breath and hopin' for the best –

JOLENE. It will be the best –

LORETTA. Cos ya might feel like a million dollars at the minute –

JOLENE. I do –

LORETTA. But ya've to prepare yaself to feel like a penny, like shite –

JOLENE. Why?

LORETTA. Cos that's what it feels like –

ABIGAIL. That's not true.

Beat.

LORETTA. Sorry?

ABIGAIL. She never has to feel like shite.

LORETTA. What's that meant to mean?

ABIGAIL. I'm just sayin' –

LORETTA (*to* JOLENE). She's only jealous cos she'll not be
the only one livin' the high life –

ABIGAIL. I'm not –

LORETTA. She'll not be able to look down her nose at ya any
more –

ABIGAIL. I don't look down my nose –

JOLENE. Ya don't, do ya?

LORETTA. Please. The only sense we ever get from her is how
technicoloured her life is – (*To* ABIGAIL.) ya dotin'
husband, ya shiny taps, clean sheets –

JOLENE. Well, why can't I have that, too?

ABIGAIL. I never said that – (*Snaps, to* LORETTA.) Ya're a
bloody liar –

LORETTA (*snaps*). Don't dare talk to me like that.

If ya made as much effort on ya knees in the bedroom as ya
do in the bathroom, ya'd have no complaints, Charlie's
words, not mine.

JOLENE. All I've ever wanted is a home, nice things –

ABIGAIL (*to* JOLENE). I know ya have – (*To* LORETTA.)
stop twistin' it –

LORETTA. I think you've said enough, Abigail.

ABIGAIL (*shouts*). I've not –

LORETTA (*shouts*). I think ya wanna shut up and stop ruinin'
ya nana's night.

Beat.

JOLENE (*to* ABIGAIL). Does my quest for happiness bore ya,
is that it?

LORETTA. Why don't ya nip across camp, fill your
Christopher in on the brilliant little birthday party I'm tossin'
ya nana?

JOLENE (*snaps*, *to* ABIGAIL). Does it?

ABIGAIL. Never. It never would –

LORETTA. He'll be so excited and rightly so, all his
Christmases, they've just come at once with you, haven't
they?

JOLENE. They have.

BARBARA. Don't dawdle, though, ya Auntie Paula'll be here
any minute.

JOLENE. I won't.

ABIGAIL. Jolene?

LORETTA. Score uz some Blu-Tack while ya out, will ya?

JOLENE. Aye.

ABIGAIL. I don't mind comin' with ya?

Exit JOLENE.

LORETTA (*to* ABIGAIL). What's your fuckin' problem?

ABIGAIL. I was only makin' conversation –

LORETTA. Ya were makin' threats.

ABIGAIL. I wasn't, I'm sorry.

BARBARA. Do ya think we should try Paula again?

ABIGAIL. I just meant she doesn't have to feel like that, no one
does –

BARBARA. She'll've got that voicemail by now, surely.

LORETTA. All that lass have ever wanted is to be wanted.

BARBARA. Loretta?

ABIGAIL. That's all I want for her, happiness –

BARBARA. Show uz how to work ya phone, I'll ring her –

LORETTA. Fuckin' hell, Mam, I'm doin' it –

BARBARA. Well, go on then –

LORETTA. She's on her way.

BARBARA. We need to be ready for her, she'll not wanna walk into this –

LORETTA. Into what?

BARBARA. You bein' like this –

LORETTA. And what's that meant to mean?

BARBARA. It's not meant to mean anythin', it's meant to mean ya wanna get ya bloody groove on, get them balloons up if ya say ya gonna –

LORETTA. I am –

BARBARA. Put the cake out, do ya banners, do anythin', look at ya, stood there like a peach –

LORETTA. Excuse me for makin' a fuckin' effort –

ABIGAIL. It doesn't matter, Nana, she's comin' and that's what counts –

LORETTA. Alright –

ABIGAIL. It does, though, cos it must be takin' a lot for her –

LORETTA (*snaps*). Fuck off –

LORETTA *grabs at balloons and banners with no real purpose.*

BARBARA. Well, go on then –

LORETTA. I'm waitin' on Blu-Tack –

BARBARA. There's always somethin' with you.

LORETTA. Always somethin' wrong, accordin' to you.

BARBARA. I never said that –

LORETTA. It's all ya say.

BARBARA. Well, cry me a river, what do ya want?

LORETTA. For you to have a nice time.

BARBARA. Don't do yaself a disservice, this isn't nice, this is wonderful, I couldn't've wished for anythin' better –

LORETTA. Alright –

ABIGAIL. It is, it's lovely, Mam –

BARBARA. Why would I wanna be sat in a restaurant when I could be here?

LORETTA. That wasn't my fault –

BARBARA. Why would I wanna feel special when I could be sat here?

LORETTA. It is special –

ABIGAIL. Dead special –

BARBARA (*snaps*). Why would I want anythin' other than you?

LORETTA (*snaps*). Cos I'm ya daughter and I'm fuckin' tryin'.

Beat.

BARBARA. Fifty balloons and a glass of cava?

LORETTA. Ya love cava –

BARBARA. I'd swap all the balloons in the world for our Paula right now.

Beat.

LORETTA. Is that supposed to tell us how much ya love her?

BARBARA. I've always loved her –

LORETTA. Why can't ya just say that then?

BARBARA. Cos she's not here –

Enter JOLENE. *She bolts through the door, throws herself on one of the beds, breaks her heart, as:*

ABIGAIL. What's happened?

JOLENE. He's said he might not be able to come –

LORETTA (*to* BARBARA). If she doesn't come, it's not the end of the world.

BARBARA (*to* LORETTA). I'm only here for her –

JOLENE. He might have to work – (*Screams.*) I don't wanna talk about it.

LORETTA (*to* BARBARA). It's took ya fourteen year to bother –

JOLENE. He's gonna bin uz off, isn't he?

BARBARA (*to* LORETTA). Don't dare talk to me like that.

ABIGAIL *grabs* JOLENE, *holds her.*

ABIGAIL. Calm down –

JOLENE. I think I'm havin' a panic attack –

LORETTA (*to* BARBARA). Tonight isn't about Paula, it's about us bein' together, surely –

JOLENE. What if he doesn't love uz?

BARBARA (*to* LORETTA). What would I want with any of you without Paula?

ABIGAIL. Then he doesn't matter.

JOLENE. He's my fiancé –

BARBARA (*to* LORETTA). What time did she leave?

JOLENE. I can't breathe –

LORETTA (*to* BARBARA). She never said –

ABIGAIL. We could always go, if ya want –

BARBARA (*to* LORETTA). Was she comin' from Edinburgh?

JOLENE. To see Christopher?

LORETTA (*to* BARBARA). I don't know.

ABIGAIL. We could leave?

BARBARA (*to* LORETTA). Why don't ya know?

LORETTA (*to* ABIGAIL). Ya goin' nowhere, either of ya –

ABIGAIL. We can do anythin' we want –

BARBARA (*to* LORETTA). Why don't ya know, Loretta?

LORETTA (*to* ABIGAIL). This isn't your night to ruin –

BARBARA (*screams*). Without Paula, tonight's worth nothin' –

LORETTA (*screams*). She's not even comin' –

I've not invited her –

*The door handle rattles, someone trying to get in as
everyone looks to the door, leading us into the next scene.*

Scene Two

1996.

Saturday 20th July. AUNTIE PAULA*'s hen night.*

BARBARA, *fifty-six, and* LORETTA, *thirty-four, are at the chalet door.* ABIGAIL, *sixteen, and* JOLENE, *fourteen, are sitting on the bed.* ABIGAIL *has a Casio keyboard on her knee.*

They are all poised with a paper cup of Pomagne. There are two suitcases downstage centre.

PAULA, *twenty-nine, off, tries the door but can't make it work.*

PAULA (*off, shouts*). Can one of ya just give it a pull?

> LORETTA *yanks the door open.*

ALL (*screams*). Happy hen night –

> *As they scream, a shit CD player comes to life on the dresser, pumps out killer hen-night tracks throughout the scene, the Spice Girls, Chesney Hawkes, Wham!, that sort of garish trash.*

> PAULA *looks baffled as* LORETTA *thrusts a Pomagne into her hand, holds her arms out, smiles wide.*

LORETTA. Paula?

> PAULA *walks uncomfortably into* LORETTA*'s hug.*
> LORETTA *'growls'.*

Where've ya been?

> PAULA *holds up a bag of Monster Munch.*

PAULA. How'd ya get here?

BARBARA. I've only had a sausage roll all day –

LORETTA *snatches the crisps from* PAULA, *tosses them to* BARBARA.

Thanks, Paula –

BARBARA *opens them, eats them over the next section.*

LORETTA. Howay then, what we missed?

JOLENE. Abigail was sick in her mouth and swallowed it.

ABIGAIL. Only cos I saw someone kick a hedgehog over a fence.

LORETTA. Well, that's a start, but it's hardly a hen night.

PAULA. Did ya get the train?

LORETTA. We drove, didn't we, Mam, like Thelma and Louise?

BARBARA. Stuck behind a caravan for the best part of the A1, listenin' to Take That on repeat –

JOLENE. What is it with you and Take That?

LORETTA. They transport uz to a higher plane –

PAULA. And here ya are –

LORETTA. And, Bob's ya uncle, here we are –

LORETTA *and* BARBARA *take in the room.*

BARBARA. This chalet takes uz back –

LORETTA. What a fuckin' shithole.

PAULA. We're only here two nights.

LORETTA. I could've brought a Glade PlugIn, if ya'd said, would've lifted the stench of stale sex out the air.

LORETTA *rubs her finger along the surfaces, sniffs them, as:*

The bathroom as rancid as out here, is it?

JOLENE. There was a crow in the toilet when we got here –

LORETTA. There never was –

JOLENE. Abigail had to fish it out with the wire from one of Paula's bras.

LORETTA. Was it dead?

ABIGAIL. It had no eyes.

LORETTA. Alright, Abigail, we've got the gist.

JOLENE. We've no hot water but they give us a travel kettle at reception.

LORETTA. To fill a bath, ya'll be there all fuckin' day.

JOLENE. We've just been havin' stand-up washes, haven't we?

ABIGAIL. Cat washes, I call them.

LORETTA. Get you, Pussy Galore.

ABIGAIL. The wardrobe door doesn't close either and there's all these little brown dots on the carpet –

PAULA. We're makin' do, though, aren't we, lasses?

LORETTA. We're on the other side of camp, not popped our heads in yet, have we, Mam, thought we'd come and surprise you lot first.

BARBARA. That's alright, isn't it?

PAULA. Ya've certainly caught uz off guard.

LORETTA. Come on then, update your nearest and dearest, what's the plan? Basically, have we to expect a stripper and, if so, when and how many?

PAULA. We've not a plan, we're just playin' it by ear –

JOLENE. We're meetin' the lasses from Paula's work in that Mexican-themed shithole for drinks.

LORETTA. That's Abigail out, she retches at the Old El Paso advert.

PAULA. I thought a couple of quiet drinks in there and that's it, nowt special, not too late a one –

ABIGAIL. Ya didn't say The Camp Champ's Championship.

BARBARA. What's that when it's at home?

LORETTA. Ignore her, it'll be somethin' shite.

PAULA. It's not something shite, actually –

ABIGAIL. I'm so nervous I could take flight –

PAULA. And rightly so –

LORETTA. Sounds like the hen night equivalent of beige so far, no offence.

PAULA. None taken.

Beat.

LORETTA. Well?

PAULA. Why don't ya pop along and see ya room and we can rendezvous with you and the others in a bit?

BARBARA. Why don't ya come with us, Paula?

LORETTA. Seems pointless now we're here, we might as well get ready with yous –

ABIGAIL. I'm doin' 'Don't Let the Sun Go Down on Me' –

LORETTA. For?

ABIGAIL. The Camp Champ's, the gay Elton John version not the George Michael one, that's the right one isn't it, ya favourite one?

JOLENE. Have ya heard her, Mam?

LORETTA. On that Casio?

PAULA. She reduces Gavin to tears with that one off the Hovis advert –

LORETTA. Ya know, I dunno if that is stale sex I'm pickin' up or Body Shop White Musk.

Is that you, Mam?

ABIGAIL. It's me.

JOLENE. How do you know what White Musk is?

ABIGAIL. I saw a lass at school with some –

LORETTA. Wait till ya see what we got –

> LORETTA *unzips her suitcase, whips out a pack of plastic-cock straws.*

Ya seen these, Paula, I'd never seen them, Cock Straws.

BARBARA. We've Cock Chocs somewhere as well.

PAULA. It's not really that kind of night –

LORETTA. Of course it's that kind of night, it's a hen night, did they go in your bag, Mam, the Cock Chocs?

BARBARA. I think so. (*To* PAULA.) We popped to Ann Summers en route.

PAULA. I'd never've guessed.

LORETTA. Ya wanna give it a whirl, Paula, they had everythin' ya'd ever want all under one roof, like Toys R Us but filth.

BARBARA. I picked up what I thought was a cordless phone, didn't I, Loretta?

LORETTA. Aye, but it was only a fuckin' dildo, wasn't it?

BARBARA. Ya should've seen my face –

LORETTA. Stood there tryin' to punch our Susan's number into its knackers.

BARBARA. The lass on the till didn't know where to look –

> LORETTA *whips out a pile of T-shirts, hands one to* PAULA.

LORETTA. I will just warn ya, he did make a slight mistake with what I said I wanted puttin' on these but, if anythin', I think it adds to them, I'll let you be the judge –

> PAULA *unfolds a T-shirt which has 'Paul's Hen Night' splashed across the front in pretty pink glitter print.*

JOLENE. Who's Paul?

PAULA. I wasn't gonna do T-shirts –

LORETTA. Then it's a good job I had the foresight to get this lot printed.

PAULA. When did ya get them done?

LORETTA. Where?

PAULA. When?

LORETTA. Just now, on the way, I can always take them back if ya'd rather be ungrateful about it –

JOLENE. They're classy as shit, Mam.

LORETTA. I know they are.

BARBARA. We showed the lass in The Jolly Roger Lounge, didn't we?

PAULA. How long ya been here?

LORETTA. Barely a couple of hours, thought we'd have a swift one for old time's sake, Mam's pissed –

PAULA. Are ya?

BARBARA. I'm not pissed, I'm in the zone.

LORETTA. We met a lovely little redcoat in there, though, didn't we, Mam?

BARBARA. Looked like Phillip Schofield before his hair went.

LORETTA. Asked if we were about later for a lock-in up The Redcoats' Bar –

BARBARA. It's an exclusive bar for redcoats, Paula, The Redcoats' Bar –

LORETTA. Fifty pence off each and every colour Breezer.

PAULA. What did you say?

LORETTA. I said, Marvin, love, that was his name, Redcoat Marvin, Marvin, love, we're on a schedule that'd put a nail-bomber to shame, but –

BARBARA. She was like a tramp on hot chips.

PAULA. I can imagine.

LORETTA. He said it's the best place to go since half the camps shut, havin' some kind of radical revamp –

BARBARA. They're gettin' a new rollercoaster and a death-defyin' log flume –

LORETTA. Fast-food outlets and a Clarks concession, that sort of upmarket shit.

PAULA. They said on reception it'd be quite a quiet weekend, I said, that'll suit me down to the ground –

JOLENE. I said it was like a ghost town but not as spooky, didn't I?

ABIGAIL. I wouldn't like it if it was too spooky.

LORETTA. You follow through watchin' Scooby-Doo.

ABIGAIL. The Manhattan Show Bar's still open –

LORETTA. Wall-to-wall ballroom dancin' in there, he said, they've not even Scampi Fries behind the bar.

ABIGAIL. It's not, it's beautiful –

LORETTA. How nice is this? All of us together like this thanks to me?

Beat.

PAULA. It's perfect.

I'm glad ya changed ya mind about comin'.

LORETTA. We never really changed it, did we, Mam?

PAULA. All for stayin' at home, last I heard –

LORETTA. Ya never really invited us, though, did ya, not proper?

BARBARA. But here we are, we're invited now, aren't we, Paula?

LORETTA. Still, though.

PAULA. It was more for the lasses from work than me, they couldn't make the one I had a fortnight back in town –

LORETTA. And how's that your problem?

PAULA. Well, they're good lasses and, I thought, what better opportunity to spend some quality time with Abigail and Jolene before –

LORETTA. And me and ya mam, of course.

PAULA. And you and Mam, course.

BARBARA. Course.

Beat.

PAULA (*to* BARBARA). Will Dad be alright with you here?

BARBARA. There's a documentary on breast implants he's been lookin' forward to all week.

PAULA. He'll be in his element.

BARBARA. He'll only be watchin' it for the nipples.

PAULA. Right.

BARBARA. He thinks it's porn –

LORETTA. Do ya mind, Paula, we're tryin' to be raucous here?

JOLENE. We're havin' a brilliant time, aren't we, Abigail?

ABIGAIL. I'm havin' the time of my life like *Dirty Dancin'*.

PAULA. And ya're here now so let's all just get on with it –

LORETTA. That's all we're tryin' to do, Paula.

Little top-up now we've somethin' saucy to sip them through?

Everyone holds out their cup.

LORETTA *tops up their Pomagne over the next section, darts a Cock Straw in with the fizz as she does.*

When ya pissin' off to Edinburgh, then?

ABIGAIL. Next weekend –

LORETTA. I was actually askin' Paula.

PAULA. Right after the weddin', I thought there's no point hangin' about.

BARBARA. Gavin'll be goin', is he?

PAULA. I'm hardly gonna leave him in Newcastle.

ABIGAIL. The new house is beautiful, have ya seen the pictures?

LORETTA. I've never been offered any pictures.

BARBARA. I have –

JOLENE. It's like somethin' out a magazine –

ABIGAIL. All them colours and patterns and possibilities –

PAULA. It's nowt special.

BARBARA. Has Gavin found a job yet or is he still contemplatin' the dole?

PAULA. He's applied for hundreds.

BARBARA. But he's not actually been offered a one?

PAULA. Worst case, it takes him a month or two, I'll be bringin' in, it's a good wage –

LORETTA. Bully for you and ya good wage.

PAULA. I've worked hard for that job.

BARBARA. Accountants are ten a penny, it's just posh maths.

PAULA. Aye, course it is.

LORETTA. That ya honeymoon, then, is it? Edinburgh, Scotland?

PAULA. We've a week in Malaga booked for the end of the month.

BARBARA. I cannet understand a word they say, the Scotch.

JOLENE. Malaga's meant to be mental in a good way –

BARBARA. All I hear's white noise.

JOLENE. I know a lass what went –

LORETTA (*to* PAULA). You won't last five minutes in Malaga with your constitution.

JOLENE. She come back with the Spanish version of malaria but still speaks very highly of it –

LORETTA. See?

BARBARA. Fat, though, isn't he?

PAULA. Gavin's not fat.

BARBARA. I wouldn't wanna give him a fireman's lift.

LORETTA. No one's askin' ya to.

BARBARA. I, for one, cannet see his appeal, there, I've said it –

PAULA. It's a good job you're not marryin' him, then, isn't it?

BARBARA. I just don't know what's so special about him –

PAULA. What do ya mean, 'what's so special about him'?

BARBARA. Why him?

PAULA. I love him.

BARBARA (*to* LORETTA). Twice last week he made Paula a cup of tea and not me.

PAULA. He's not a teasmaid.

BARBARA. No, but manners cost nowt, ya dad's words, not mine.

LORETTA. Does he stay over?

BARBARA. He's there more than I am and I'm always there.

PAULA. He's not stayed the night.

BARBARA. Stays till all hours, though, doesn't he, heavy-pettin' on my good cushion covers, don't think I've not heard ya slobberin' –

PAULA. Well, ya'll not have to put up with it much longer, will ya?

BARBARA. It's him that offends uz, not you, you can stay for life for me.

LORETTA. She's already said, she's goin' –

BARBARA. I've never been alone in that house.

PAULA. Ya've got Dad.

BARBARA. Exactly.

Beat.

ABIGAIL. I'll come round all the time, Nana, we can watch *Fifteen to One* –

LORETTA. Does anyone else's cock taste funny?

BARBARA. Mine's fine.

LORETTA. They're maybes flavoured, I should've checked –

ABIGAIL *presses the demo button on her Casio and it blares out.*

LORETTA *shits herself, screams.*

I almost had an epileptic fit.

ABIGAIL. I just knocked it –

LORETTA. Well, can ya just unknock it, please, it's a fuckin' hindrance.

PAULA. She's alright – (*To* ABIGAIL.) Do ya wanna do another practice run for ya mam?

LORETTA. How's about we whack them T-shirts on?

JOLENE. Can I go first, Mam, I love fashion.

PAULA. I don't want any fuss.

LORETTA. It's ya last night of freedom, ya wanna aim for the stars.

PAULA. I'm not goin' to jail.

LORETTA. I was shittin' blood the day after my hen night.

PAULA. As appealin' as that is, I'm happy with a quiet one.

LORETTA. There's plenty of time to be quiet when ya dead.

PAULA. I'm really gonna miss our little chats –

LORETTA. Well, at least have a Cock Choc –

PAULA. Fine.

LORETTA. Howay, Mam, fish them out – (*To* PAULA.)
They've a lemon-fondant centre to emulate semen.

BARBARA *unzips her case, quickly slams it shut.*

JOLENE. What's wrong?

BARBARA. I've a surprise for Paula.

PAULA. Howay, then –

BARBARA. I was gonna give it ya later, I had it all planned
out –

LORETTA. Well, give it her later, then.

BARBARA. But I wanna give it her now, I'm excited now –

LORETTA. Well, give it her now, then.

BARBARA. I think I wanna wait.

LORETTA. I told ya she was pissed.

BARBARA. I want it to be special.

LORETTA. Well, at least pass the Cock Chocs – (*To* PAULA.)
It's like care in the fuckin' community.

PAULA. She's doin' no one any harm –

BARBARA *peers into her suitcase, rifles around for what
feels like for ever, looks puzzled.*

BARBARA. I think I've left them in the car.

LORETTA. I wish I'd left you in the bloody car.

BARBARA. I'm so sorry, Paula – (*To* LORETTA.) Will I go and get them?

LORETTA. Don't bother, the moment's gone.

If they melt and that lemon semen leaks all over my beaded seat cover, it'll be you that walks to Halfords to replace it.

Been gettin' a new top, Jolene?

JOLENE. It's Paula's.

PAULA. It's only a cheap one off the market –

LORETTA. I've the exact same one with a streak of silver up the tits, mine's not market, though, I find they tend to unravel after a couple of washes.

PAULA. I don't find that.

LORETTA. Still, I'd rather pay the extra for New Look.

BARBARA. I like your jumper, Abigail.

ABIGAIL. It's my best jumper, Nana.

LORETTA. She's never out of it.

PAULA. I'm not surprised, it's gorgeous.

LORETTA (*to* ABIGAIL). Ya wanna flash a bit of skin now and again, pop ya best goods out front like a greengrocer.

ABIGAIL. I haven't any goods.

LORETTA. Take a leaf out ya sister's book and ya might get a boyfriend. (*To* BARBARA.) She's a wardrobe full of halter necks she'll not even try on.

PAULA. There's no rush.

LORETTA. If anyone's a use-by date, it's her.

BARBARA. Still not got a fancy man, Abigail?

LORETTA. The closest thing she's had to a snog is a lick off next door's dog.

ABIGAIL. It's not.

LORETTA. And even he knocked her back for a lick of his own arse –

PAULA. Alright, Loretta.

BARBARA. Have you a fancy man, Jolene?

JOLENE. Aye, Luke, he's gorgeous, Nana, isn't he, Mam?

LORETTA. He's like somethin' out of *Beverly Hills 90210*, I've told him he wants to get himself into catalogue modellin', he's such lovely sleek curtains.

JOLENE. We're totally gettin' married.

LORETTA. And I couldn't be bloody prouder.

BARBARA. Ya'll have to bring him round one time for his tea, what's he like with cod in a bag?

ABIGAIL. Did ya know Paula's Gavin used to be a model?

BARBARA. For what, Evans?

PAULA. He wasn't technically a model.

LORETTA. What 'technically' was he, then?

ABIGAIL. The Milky Bar Kid.

LORETTA. He doesn't even wear glasses.

BARBARA. Explains why he's so rotund, though, some folk never drop their puppy fat.

PAULA. Will ya leave it?

LORETTA *pinches* ABIGAIL*'s cheek.*

LORETTA. We've livin' proof right here, haven't we?

JOLENE. I'd love to have Abigail's figure.

LORETTA. I wouldn't thank ya for it –

PAULA. Don't be such a bitch –

LORETTA. I'm not, but look at her, all twisted up like a bloody Quaver.

(*To* ABIGAIL.) If ya held yaself up straight, ya'd not have so many confidence issues –

ABIGAIL *presses the demo button on her Casio and it blares out.*

And I dunno why ya've brought that – (*To* PAULA.) Mornin', noon and bastard night I have to put up with this –

LORETTA *snatches the Casio from* ABIGAIL, *shoves it behind a pillow.*

ABIGAIL. I need it for tonight –

LORETTA. What do ya need it for tonight for?

PAULA. She's told ya, The Camp Champ's Championship, do ya not listen?

LORETTA. Only when there's somethin' worth listenin' to.

ABIGAIL. I've been practisin' weeks.

BARBARA. What's this she's ravin' on about?

JOLENE. The Camp Champ's Championship, we're goin' tonight –

LORETTA. We're bloody not.

ABIGAIL. Paula promised –

LORETTA. I've not come all this way to watch you balance on a ball like a dancin' fuckin' bear.

ABIGAIL. I'm not dancin', I'm playin' ya song –

LORETTA. What time we meetin' these lasses, Paula?

PAULA. Half seven.

LORETTA. And who are they, tell uz their names?

PAULA. Mandy and Fiona from the office, ya don't know them –

JOLENE. They're lush, Mam, we all went for tea last night, Fiona's dead clever –

LORETTA. I've not even met the lass and she's already boilin' my piss.

ABIGAIL. She's gonna be a doctor of children's books –

LORETTA. She wants to read a proper book, what's that one I give you, Mam?

BARBARA. The Barbara Taylor Bradford?

LORETTA. *A Woman of Substance*, now that's a book, that's romance right there. I give it to Claude to have a finger through, pick up a few tips on elevatin' himself to the sexual realms of a tall, dark and handsome stranger –

BARBARA. Did he not bite?

LORETTA. When it comes to the bedroom, he's as much use as a fuckin' humidifier –

BARBARA. Is it any wonder when ya've breasts like place mats?

LORETTA. It's this top, it flattens them –

BARBARA. No wonder he'll only do ya up the back passage.

Beat.

PAULA. Is there any need for that?

BARBARA. She told uz at Gordon's weddin' when she was mortal –

LORETTA. I don't think I did –

BARBARA. Said it knacked but that ya love him –

LORETTA. I do love him.

Another drink and then we wanna start gettin' ready –

LORETTA *whips out another bottle of Pomagne from her bag.*

Everyone holds out their cup and LORETTA *tops them up over the next section.*

BARBARA. I need a wet, will someone take uz.

LORETTA. I told ya she was pissed. Abigail, take ya nana to the toilet.

BARBARA. Will you take uz, Paula?

PAULA. Ya can manage yaself, Mam, ya know ya can.

BARBARA. Well, if ya gonna take uz, take uz now, Abigail, cos I think I'm mortal.

ABIGAIL *helps* BARBARA *up, guides her up and into the bathroom.*

LORETTA. Christ, she's hard work –

BARBARA (*off, shouts*). Hard work I might be, but I'm not deaf –

PAULA (*shouts*). Shut up, Mam.

(*To* JOLENE.) Where's your Luke this weekend then?

JOLENE. Center Parcs, I'm missin' him so much, he makes uz feel like I'm made of stars.

LORETTA. There's nowt so lush as young love, is there, Paula?

PAULA (*to* JOLENE). If only ya could bottle it.

They drink.

LORETTA. I wish I could say the same about Claude, but he'd not even crossed my mind till that bag of bones brought him up –

ABIGAIL *enters, takes a seat.*

ABIGAIL. She's fine.

PAULA. Good lass. (*To* LORETTA.) What's happened?

LORETTA. He's started takin' care of himself.

PAULA. That's surely a good thing.

LORETTA. I don't just mean havin' a bath and brushin' his teeth, it's more than that –

PAULA. What?

LORETTA. I think he's seein' someone else –

LORETTA *breaks down.*

PAULA. What's all this?

LORETTA. He's started wearin' aftershave, Paula, vests and dog tags, spikin' his hair up like Sonic the Hedgehog.

JOLENE. It's all the rage at the minute, Mam –

LORETTA. He said this mornin' that he was thinkin' about gettin' his ear pierced, there's a diamante stud in Argos he won't stop ravin' on about and last week, last week –

PAULA. What?

LORETTA. He trimmed his pubes.

PAULA. On his own?

LORETTA. With my good scissors –

She sobs.

He doesn't look at uz the same.

It's like I've give him my heart and he's swingin' it round his head in a Tesco bag.

Silence. No one knows what to say.

LORETTA *composes herself, drinks.*

I'm sorry, it's nowt, ignore uz –

It's just that I love him so much, it's stupid, I know, but –

ABIGAIL. Men are shit, Mam –

LORETTA. Go and check on ya nana.

ABIGAIL. Cos love is only ever part of a man's life –

LORETTA (*to* PAULA). Ya heard this?

ABIGAIL. But love's a woman's whole existence.

Beat.

LORETTA. And what would you know about anythin'?

Too much bloody Pomagne, that's my trouble, I shouldn't't've started on pints, ya know what I'm like –

LORETTA *goes to the mirror, stares at herself, wipes her mascara eyes.*

Panda eyes.

PAULA. They're soon fixed.

LORETTA. Course. Where he lets uz down, mascara lifts uz back up.

Over the next section, LORETTA *reapplies her eye make-up.*

What ya doin' with ya hair on the day?

PAULA. I'm gonna crimp it.

LORETTA. Ya wanna ask Spacker Karen, she did Kevin's wife for Christine's funeral and she looked like somethin' out of *Clash of the Titans*, in a good way, obviously.

JOLENE. Spacker Karen does everyone at school for school disco.

PAULA. I've already booked Cut-and-Blow-Dry Margaret.

LORETTA. Either way, we'll be round first thing with the flowers so, worst case, she's as shite as everyone reckons, I'll do ya myself.

JOLENE. I'll help ya, Mam –

LORETTA *turns round, she's done, her face firmly in place.*

LORETTA. I can't wait for tonight, it's ages since I've had a good girly night out, years since I've put this world to rights.

ABIGAIL. When I do ya song, if I get it right, I'm hopin' it'll take ya to the places Take That take ya.

LORETTA. Ya might have the same moustache as little Mark Owen but I doubt very much ya wanna take uz to the places he does –

ABIGAIL. I can try –

LORETTA. Cos, and I know I should've checked with ya first, Paula.

PAULA. What?

LORETTA. But I said to that Marvin, Redcoat Marvin, that we would meet him later –

Enter BARBARA.

BARBARA. That stench has knocked us for six –

JOLENE. It'll be that dead crow –

LORETTA. Nowt to do with the umpteen rum and Cokes?

PAULA. I've half a strip of Rennies, if ya want a one?

BARBARA. They give uz indigestion.

PAULA. Right –

LORETTA. I said that I said we would meet Marvin, Redcoat Marvin.

BARBARA. Ya'll love him, Paula, he's this big, round, shiny face.

PAULA. I'll have to check with Mandy and Fiona –

LORETTA. It's nowt to do with them –

PAULA. I don't wanna be late, not with the girls –

JOLENE. I don't mind.

LORETTA. Fifty pence off each and every colour Breezer, Paula, it's the kind of thing no one says no to.

JOLENE. Please, Paula?

Beat.

PAULA. I suppose.

LORETTA. I suggested he bring a little friend as well.

JOLENE. What little friend?

LORETTA. Redcoat Max, the unfashionable but not-completely-unfortunate-lookin' thing he had trailin' after him –

PAULA. What for?

LORETTA. A little date with Abigail.

(*To* ABIGAIL.) Surprise.

ABIGAIL. Me?

LORETTA *sits next to* ABIGAIL, *tops up her drink, smiles at her.*

LORETTA. He's only in trainin' but a redcoat all the same.

ABIGAIL. I'm alright –

LORETTA. Ya wanna be a big girl, don't ya? Ya wanna be included?

PAULA. She is included, come on, let's get these T-shirts on –

PAULA *picks up a T-shirt, puts it on.*

LORETTA. Ya want uz to be proud of ya, don't ya?

ABIGAIL. Course I do.

PAULA *twirls.*

PAULA. What do ya reckon?

JOLENE. Ya'd pay three quid for that in a shop.

PAULA. Loretta?

LORETTA. Ya cannet hide yaself away ya whole life, ya've a half decent pair of tits, I dunno why ya so intent on coverin' yaself up –

ABIGAIL. Cos I'm a state.

LORETTA. Then we'll give ya a little makeover, ya'll not recognise yaself –

ABIGAIL. I want to recognise myself.

PAULA. Loretta, what are ya doin'?

JOLENE. Can I do her make-up?

LORETTA. There ya go, look how excited ya sister is.

PAULA. We've got plans, we're goin' out –

LORETTA. Course we are, we're all goin' out.

JOLENE. I'll do bright-red lips ya can't help but wanna snog off –

BARBARA. Ya wanna get yaself a job in Boots the Chemist, Jolene.

ABIGAIL. Do I have to snog?

PAULA. No, ya don't. Loretta, can I have a word outside –

LORETTA. This is your night to do whatever ya heart desires, whatever it is ya want, stand up straight and be counted –

LORETTA *drags* ABIGAIL *up to the mirror, pulls her hair up and away from her face.*

Look how lovely ya could be if ya really really really tried.

PAULA. She is lovely –

LORETTA. Can ya see it?

ABIGAIL *nods.*

Come on, then –

Hop to it, Jolene –

Over the next section, LORETTA *and* JOLENE *tend to* ABIGAIL*'s hair and make-up.*

PAULA *removes her hen-night T-shirt.*

PAULA. This isn't the night we had planned –

LORETTA. I know it's not, no mention of me and Mam in ya plan, ya've made that perfectly clear. (*To* JOLENE.) Lip-line and then fill.

PAULA. It wasn't like that –

BARBARA. Fair point, well made, Loretta.

PAULA. Let's go for a drink, Mam'll watch the girls –

LORETTA. I'm fine here.

PAULA. If ya right about Claude, this isn't the way –

LORETTA. Tell her how made up ya are, Abigail –

PAULA. Abigail?

Beat.

ABIGAIL. I cannet hide myself away my whole life, Paula.

LORETTA. Straight from the horse's mouth. (*To* JOLENE.) Less line, more fill.

JOLENE. Ya'll have such lovely skin.

ABIGAIL. Will I?

PAULA. Then let's just hang out here for a bit, we can hook up with the lasses from the office any time –

LORETTA. Half seven, you said. (*To* JOLENE.) And pile that foundation on to soak up the grease.

PAULA. Anywhere ya want but not like this –

JOLENE. Look at her comin' to life, Mam.

BARBARA. Ya finally startin' to look bonny.

ABIGAIL. Am I?

JOLENE. Like a young Meg Ryan.

BARBARA. Which one's she?

PAULA (*snaps*). Loretta –

LORETTA. Back up, Jolene – (*To* ABIGAIL.) Let uz look at ya –

ABIGAIL *tries to stand up straight, be someone else.*

I'm thinkin' sultry and I'm thinkin' thigh-high –

JOLENE. Totally, Mam.

LORETTA. Let's get ya out of this lot first, though – (*To* JOLENE.) Give her a hand –

JOLENE *undresses* ABIGAIL *to her knickers and bra,* PAULA *tries to stop her, grabbing at* ABIGAIL*'s clothes.*

PAULA. This is disgustin' –

ABIGAIL. My body?

PAULA. No, not ya body –

JOLENE. She's just gettin' ready like any normal person, Paula.

PAULA (*to* JOLENE). Leave her –

LORETTA (*to* PAULA). Back off –

ABIGAIL. It's fine, Paula, really. It's fine.

> PAULA *steps back,* LORETTA *rifles through* JOLENE's
> *suitcase for a dress.*

LORETTA. Arms up and ready, Abigail –

> ABIGAIL *raises her arms, ready for a dress to be dropped*
> *onto her, keeps them there, as:*

ABIGAIL. There's this lad I like at school called Shane.

> He's one of the more popular boys, he plays the flute in the
> school band, even though it's a dead puffy instrument.

> I'd love to be in that band, once my Casio skills pick up,
> once I can transfer to piano properly and play dead
> wonderful tunes for Shane to hear.

LORETTA. Ya say that, pet, but if this Shane is one of the more
popular boys, he's more than likely gonna wanna have nowt
to do with you, is he?

ABIGAIL. No.

LORETTA (*to* JOLENE). Blend her eyes out a bit, she looks
positively gaunt.

PAULA. Why wouldn't he?

> LORETTA *whips out a short dress, low-cut, vile.*

LORETTA. Here –

> (*To* JOLENE.) Move –

> LORETTA *drops the dress onto* ABIGAIL, *pulls it into*
> *place,* ABIGAIL *squirms, as:*

JOLENE. It's not Shane Orange, is it?

ABIGAIL. Aye.

JOLENE. He's riddled.

BARBARA. What is he?

JOLENE. He's the one that give Wendy with the fur coat chlamydia.

LORETTA. Well, there ya go, ya want nowt to do with him or his flute now we've ascertained where he's been stickin' it.

BARBARA. I've a lovely fur coat in the loft, if anyone wants it?

LORETTA (*to* ABIGAIL). Stand still –

(*To* JOLENE.) Carry on while I take her in –

LORETTA *steps back, takes in* ABIGAIL *as* JOLENE *continues with her make-up.*

She looks somehow incomplete.

JOLENE. Have we time for a French plait?

LORETTA. I'm too pissed for a French plait.

JOLENE. How do ya feel, Abigail?

Beat.

ABIGAIL. I feel like the Little Mermaid when she gets her legs.

LORETTA *looks proud as rum punch.*

LORETTA. Did ya hear that, everyone? Paula?

PAULA. I heard.

LORETTA (*to* JOLENE). That's enough now, get gone –

(*To* ABIGAIL.) Go on –

ABIGAIL. This is all I've ever wanted.

Cos I can glitter even though I'm not gold.

JOLENE. Bless.

LORETTA. I know, bless.

I appreciate ya sentiment, Abigail, but we're gonna have to nip down that seven-eleven for some tights, pet –

JOLENE. That's what's missin'.

LORETTA. I've never seen a set of pins so corned beefy or hairy but, apart from that, she looks alright, doesn't she, everyone?

BARBARA. She's one of ya finer efforts, Loretta.

ABIGAIL. Paula?

Beat.

PAULA. Ya look really pretty.

LORETTA. Careful not to inflate the lass's ego –

PAULA (*snaps*). What the fuck do ya want uz to say?

LORETTA (*snaps*). Nothin', shut up.

(*To* JOLENE.) We can talk about what to do with her shoes en route.

JOLENE. Did ya bring them electric-blue ones ya wore for Yvonne's last Tupperware party?

LORETTA. That's exactly what I was thinkin', black tights, blue shoes.

JOLENE. Like a little Bertie Bassett.

LORETTA (*to* JOLENE). Get ya spends, then, I've not been to the cash point – (*To* BARBARA.) Do ya want some fresh air, Mam, clear ya head?

BARBARA. I think I'm gonna be sick.

LORETTA. Howay with us, then, I reckon that toilet'll buckle under anythin' thicker than a wet –

ABIGAIL. I dunno if I'm ready.

PAULA. See?

LORETTA (*to* PAULA, *screams*). Shut. Up.

Listen, Abigail, this is what lasses do, they have fun, they talk about lads, like you just did with Shane what's-his-face, ya've never once gone on like that, never once opened up proper, have ya?

ABIGAIL *shakes her head.*

Lasses have sex, they don't sit in the corner, hunched up like a bin bag playin' on Casios and dreamin' about boys.

ABIGAIL. I know.

LORETTA. Then, ya'll be alright, won't ya? Look at ya, all dressed up with somewhere to go. Have another Pomagne to steady ya nerves, wet ya whistle, I'll not be long, blink and I'll be back –

(*To* PAULA.) I assume you're stayin' here?

PAULA. Please don't do this, Loretta –

LORETTA. I'm givin' the lass a chance –

PAULA (*snaps*). She's sixteen.

LORETTA (*snaps*). So were you when ya disappeared up Chopwell Woods with Darren Custard, problem?

PAULA (*snaps*). No.

Beat.

LORETTA. Maybe ya should come with us, Abigail?

ABIGAIL. I'm fine here.

LORETTA (*to* PAULA). Is she fine?

PAULA (*snaps*). Course she is.

LORETTA. Is she?

Beat.

PAULA. She looks really pretty, I'm pleased for her, made up for her, for her havin' this chance, really.

LORETTA. Do uz a favour, then, and help her shave her legs, we'll not be long, alright?

PAULA. Aye.

LORETTA. Come on, you pair –

BARBARA. Am I comin' with you?

LORETTA. Yes, Mam, move it –

Exit LORETTA, BARBARA *and* JOLENE.

ABIGAIL. Do you really think I look pretty?

PAULA. Aye.

ABIGAIL. What about beautiful?

PAULA. I've always told ya ya're beautiful.

ABIGAIL. I've never felt beautiful. I'm crap hair, I'm crap skin and crap dreams –

PAULA. Don't say that –

ABIGAIL. She says, not me.

PAULA. She's just upset.

ABIGAIL. I didn't do anythin' to her.

Beat.

PAULA. Here –

PAULA *holds* ABIGAIL, *clings to her like she's going out of fashion, holds her out in front of her.*

ABIGAIL. I don't like people seein' my body, let alone touchin' it.

PAULA. That's alright.

ABIGAIL. I know my mam said to shave my legs but, can ya not? I'd feel funny even you touchin' them.

PAULA. I wouldn't have –

ABIGAIL. They're only a mess cos no one ever sees them.

What if my downstairs isn't normal like other lasses?

PAULA. There's no such thing as 'normal'.

ABIGAIL. There's such a thing as sexy, though, isn't there? What if I can't be that sexy? I can't even dance.

Can you dance?

PAULA. I can do the Macarena.

ABIGAIL. What's that?

PAULA. It's a dance, admittedly, a really shit one, but –

ABIGAIL. Will ya show uz how to do it?

PAULA. I'll show ya for fun, not for any other reason.

ABIGAIL. I wanna feel like I'm havin' fun.

PAULA. Okay.

> PAULA *changes the CD in the player, skips to the track, pauses it.*

> I'll run ya through it first, you copy uz, and then we'll do it together with the music, alright?

ABIGAIL. Alright. You go in front and I'll go behind, though –

> PAULA *stands in front of* ABIGAIL *so she can't see her.*

PAULA. Loosen up, like ya haven't any bones, all floppy, like this –

> PAULA *goes all floppy.*

ABIGAIL. I cannet do that.

PAULA. This is what ya have to do, come on –

> ABIGAIL *reluctantly copies.*

> Are ya floppy back there?

ABIGAIL. Proper floppy, Paula.

PAULA. Right. Here goes nothin' –

> PAULA *narrates the Macarena as* ABIGAIL *watches intently, copies.*

> Start off by whackin' ya hands out straight in front, one at a time, like ya're chasin' away a bumble bee.

> *She demonstrates.*

> Again but flip ya hands over, like ya checkin' ya palm for stings.

> *She demonstrates.*

Criss-cross ya hands across ya chest, like ya 'kini's just snapped up the swimmin' baths and ya tits are about to pop out.

She demonstrates.

Touch ya head, like ya're gonna be sick and no one's there to hold ya hair back.

She demonstrates.

Hands to ya waist, like ya period pains are cripplin'.

She demonstrates.

Palms to ya hips, like ya're absolutely foamin', and grind.

She demonstrates.

Grind and jump and turn.

She demonstrates.

How was that?

ABIGAIL. I feel like such a tit.

PAULA. I bet ya were brilliant.

ABIGAIL. It's incredibly elaborate.

PAULA. It's much less tricky with a beat goin'. I'll tell ya when, alright?

ABIGAIL. Is this why lads love lasses?

PAULA. Basically.

> PAULA *presses play and 'Macarena' by Los del Rio blares out.*

Ready?

ABIGAIL. Ready.

The chorus kicks in.

PAULA. Now –

They dance, ABIGAIL *copying* PAULA*'s moves.*

At first she's shit but soon settles into a rhythm, is ecstatic, lets herself go, has fun, a genuine smile stretches across her face for the first time.

ABIGAIL. This is brilliant.

PAULA. I told ya.

ABIGAIL. Who told ya how to feel this good?

PAULA. I dunno.

ABIGAIL. I've never used my body like this before.

I feel fantastic –

ABIGAIL *suddenly stops dancing, freezes.*

PAULA, *being in front, doesn't notice, continues dancing, as:*

PAULA. I'll tell Gavin to put it on at the weddin' next week.

We could have a dance together, get Jolene up, maybes even ya nana, do ya reckon?

Abigail?

PAULA *eventually turns, clocks* ABIGAIL, *stops dancing.*

What's wrong?

ABIGAIL *shakes her head.*

Abigail?

ABIGAIL. Dunno.

PAULA. Of anyone, ya can tell me.

ABIGAIL. I don't ever like to tell anyone.

PAULA. Tell them what?

Will I get all this horrible mess off?

ABIGAIL *nods.*

Will I tell ya mam?

ABIGAIL *nods.*

Ya're alright.

PAULA *takes some make-up wipes from her bag, rips a few out, tenderly wipes away* ABIGAIL*'s make-up, she closes her eyes, loving it.*

Ya so bonny.

ABIGAIL *shakes her head.*

Ya are.

Beat.

ABIGAIL. Thanks for showin' uz the Macarena.

PAULA. There's better dances I can show ya.

ABIGAIL. Miss you.

PAULA. Miss you.

Beat.

ABIGAIL. Can we try it one last time, for fun again?

PAULA. Course. Come on –

PAULA *and* ABIGAIL *dance the Macarena, side by side,* ABIGAIL *stealing smiles at* PAULA.

ABIGAIL. This is my favourite time with you –

Enter LORETTA.

LORETTA. What's this?

They stop dancing.

Until indicated, ABIGAIL *keeps her back to* LORETTA, *her face hidden.*

ABIGAIL. Nothin' –

LORETTA. Were you pair doin' the Macarena?

PAULA. We were just muckin' about.

ABIGAIL. It was a bit of fun –

LORETTA. Show uz, then, how ya have fun.

ABIGAIL *shakes her head.*

I could join in?

ABIGAIL. It was nothin' –

LORETTA. If ya're good enough to show uz what to do –

ABIGAIL. I don't even know what I'm doin' –

LORETTA. It didn't look like it.

PAULA. Leave her.

LORETTA. Looked like ya knew exactly what ya were doin', do it again –

PAULA (*snaps*). Stop it –

ABIGAIL (*snaps*). No –

LORETTA (*snaps*). Come on, Abigail –

ABIGAIL *tentatively performs the Macarena, her back to* LORETTA, *she's shaking, only manages a few moves before she stops, statuesque.*

What ya stoppin' for?

PAULA. She doesn't want to go, Loretta.

ABIGAIL *turns round,* LORETTA *clocks her face, stops the CD.*

LORETTA. Someone's been busy.

ABIGAIL (*quietly*). I don't want to go –

LORETTA. What ya sayin' to me?

ABIGAIL (*louder*). I don't want to go with him –

LORETTA. I can't even hear ya –

PAULA. Are ya deaf?

ABIGAIL (*snaps*). I can't.

Beat.

LORETTA. Fetch uz that lipstick and I won't hear any
  arguments.

ABIGAIL brings LORETTA *the lipstick, she paints it onto
her, thicker than before, a mess.*

And there we go, everybody's happy.

LORETTA *hands her a pack of tights.*

Get in there and get in these, that's a good girl.

ABIGAIL *looks to* PAULA.

(*Screams.*) I said go –

Exit ABIGAIL *to the bathroom, slams the door.*

Finally, a teenage temper-tantrum –

Over the next section, LORETTA *rushes to get changed,
primped and preened.*

PAULA. Where's them pair?

LORETTA. We bumped into the lads at the seven-eleven,
  they're dawdlin' back over with them.

PAULA. Redcoat Marvin?

LORETTA. And Redcoat Max, aye.

  Have ya any Insette?

PAULA. I've not.

LORETTA. I was sure I packed a tin.

PAULA. Why aren't ya with them?

LORETTA. I've not had time to get ready, have I, spent too
  bloody long makin' sure sad-sack looks the part.

PAULA. She looks awful –

LORETTA. Says her that could do with a colour runnin'
  through her hair.

LORETTA *backcombs her hair in the mirror as:*

She's never stood a chance, our Abigail. I've not once looked at her and thought she'd be fine, thought get yaself away, do as ya please, come back and tell uz all about it.

She's different, in all the very best and bad ways –

PAULA. Ya don't have to do this.

LORETTA. I don't have to do anythin', I want to do it –

PAULA. Ya've a husband at home –

LORETTA. And fat lot of good he is, cos I dunno who it's for, but he's not spikin' his hair for me.

PAULA. Ya never know –

LORETTA. I do know, I know him. He won't talk, won't listen, he's good for nowt –

LORETTA *stops, stares at her reflection.*

I've not once had the sex I want to have.

Enter BARBARA *and* JOLENE, LORETTA *springs back to life.*

BARBARA. What are they like in their best shirts?

JOLENE. They're dead canny, aren't they, Mam?

LORETTA. They weren't canny, they're fuckin' awe-inspirin', and Max –

The bathroom door slowly opens. ABIGAIL *emerges in her tights.*

We're just sayin' about Max, Abigail. Under the glare of those fluorescent tubes up the seven-eleven, he put uz in mind of a shorter, whiter, Fresh Prince of Bel Air, what do ya think about that?

ABIGAIL *shrugs.*

Look how excited she is.

BARBARA (*to* ABIGAIL). They're just outside, have a look.

JOLENE. I said for them to give us five, are we almost ready?

LORETTA. Almost.

LORETTA *takes a condom from her make-up bag, hands it to* ABIGAIL.

ABIGAIL. What's that for?

LORETTA. Just pop it in ya pocket –

PAULA. She's not goin'.

PAULA *grabs* ABIGAIL*'s hand.*

LORETTA. And what's it got to do with you?

PAULA. She's comin' with me –

LORETTA. Doubt it.

PAULA. We're away up The Camp Champ's –

LORETTA. Are ya?

PAULA. She's gonna play her Casio –

LORETTA. Is she now?

PAULA. This is my night and I say what goes and this –

LORETTA. What?

PAULA. Doin' this to her is not, no way, happenin' –

LORETTA (*snaps*). Says who?

PAULA (*snaps*). No way –

Get ya Casio, Abigail.

LORETTA (*to* ABIGAIL). Try it.

ABIGAIL *freezes.*

PAULA (*to* ABIGAIL). Come on, love –

LORETTA (*to* ABIGAIL). You fuckin' dare.

ABIGAIL *can't move.*

PAULA *reaches behind the pillow and pulls free the Casio.*

(*Snaps.*) Give it –

PAULA (*snaps*). No –

LORETTA *tries to snatch it from her, fails.*

LORETTA. I'm warnin' ya, Paula, fuck with uz and it'll be the last thing ya fuckin' do –

PAULA *hands the Casio to* ABIGAIL*, she tentatively takes it.*

She's my daughter –

PAULA. Ya've a funny way of showin' it.

LORETTA. I love her –

ABIGAIL. Please don't fight –

LORETTA (*to* ABIGAIL). Ya know I love ya, don't ya?

This is all for you.

LORETTA *approaches* ABIGAIL*, arms outstretched, quickly snatches the Casio from her, holds it behind her back, smiles.*

PAULA. Give her it –

LORETTA. No.

PAULA (*to* BARBARA). Tell her –

BARBARA. I'm not gettin' involved.

PAULA. I'm not askin' ya to, I'm askin' ya to put ya foot down.

JOLENE. Tell her, Nana.

LORETTA. Go on, Mam –

BARBARA (*to* PAULA). She's her daughter, not mine –

PAULA. She's your fuckin' granddaughter –

BARBARA. I cannet bear the piano –

ABIGAIL (*snaps*). It's beautiful –

LORETTA (*snaps*). Don't ever snap at ya nana –

ABIGAIL. Please –

JOLENE. Give her it –

PAULA (*snaps*). It's hers –

LORETTA (*snaps*). Who paid for it?

PAULA (*screams*). It's the only thing that makes her happy –

LORETTA (*screams*). Why should she be happy –

LORETTA *smashes the Casio off the wall in a single, violent strike.*

ABIGAIL *remains completely silent but her face tells us that she has just been ripped in two.*

Game over.

PAULA. That wasn't yours to do that with –

LORETTA. I don't care –

PAULA. Well, ya fuckin' should.

PAULA *grabs* ABIGAIL.

Look at her.

LORETTA. She scrubs up a treat, ya might wanna try it.

PAULA. She's devastated –

LORETTA. She's finally comin' into her own –

PAULA. Ask her –

LORETTA (*snaps*). I don't have to ask her –

PAULA (*snaps*). She's never felt good enough for ya, Loretta –

LORETTA *grabs* ABIGAIL *back.*

LORETTA. Exactly and now she does, job done.

Beat.

PAULA. Ya're tearin' her apart –

LORETTA. Aye, and you'll be next –

PAULA. Here we go –

LORETTA. That's right –

PAULA. The drink talkin' –

LORETTA. That's me –

PAULA. Always pissed –

LORETTA. Always pissed, never anythin' else, never fuckin' good enough –

PAULA. Struck a nerve?

LORETTA. Never up to your high standards –

PAULA. And what are they?

LORETTA. You and ya fancy fuckin' job, ya child-star fiancé –

PAULA. The Milky Bar Kid?

LORETTA. Palmin' ya clothes off on my daughters, mine, Paula, like they're not good enough either –

PAULA. She said she liked it –

LORETTA. Well, ya nowt, nothin' without none of that –

PAULA. Nowt?

LORETTA. Call yaself a woman?

PAULA. You're the one gettin' bummed left, right and centre –

LORETTA (*snaps*). I do not get bummed.

It's called anal, Paula, and, if ya didn't have such a fat arse –

PAULA (*shouts*). Just say it –

Beat.

LORETTA. Why didn't ya invite us tonight?

BARBARA. Do ya want ya surprise, Paula?

LORETTA (*snaps*). Not now, Mam –

BARBARA. It's no bother –

   BARBARA *scrambles about for her suitcase, finds it, drags it out, as:*

LORETTA. Embarrassed in front of ya pals, were ya?

PAULA. That's right –

LORETTA. Worried we'd give ya game away?

PAULA. Aye –

LORETTA. That ya're all mouth and no trousers, all P's and no Q's?

PAULA. I didn't want ya here –

LORETTA. That's it –

PAULA. That's it –

LORETTA. And why not?

   (*Snaps.*) Say it.

   BARBARA *opens her suitcase.*

PAULA (*shouts*). Cos I knew ya'd ruin it.

   LORETTA *curtsies.*

LORETTA. You're very welcome.

   BARBARA *pulls free her wedding dress.*

BARBARA. Look.

   Beat.

PAULA. I've told ya, Mam, I've already got my dress.

BARBARA. But this is an heirloom –

PAULA. And it's gorgeous.

BARBARA. Then, what's wrong?

LORETTA. I wore it, Paula.

PAULA. I know ya did –

BARBARA. And that makes it tradition, doesn't it?

LORETTA. Course it does –

BARBARA. It makes it family tradition.

PAULA. We're not one of them families.

BARBARA. But we are a family and this is my surprise –

PAULA. How many times, I don't want the dress.

Beat.

LORETTA. She thinks it's not good enough.

PAULA. This doesn't involve you –

LORETTA. Thinks ya takin' the piss –

BARBARA. I thought ya'd like it –

PAULA. I do like it –

BARBARA. At least thank uz for it –

LORETTA. She's laughin' at ya, Mam –

PAULA. I dunno why ya think I have to have it –

LORETTA. Why don't ya just throw it back in her face?

Here –

LORETTA *takes the wedding dress from* BARBARA, *stands next to* PAULA *and throws it in* BARBARA*'s face.*

PAULA *pushes* LORETTA *away.*

PAULA (*to* LORETTA). Fuck off –

BARBARA *stares at the dress on the floor, doesn't take her eyes off it across the next section.*

BARBARA. I wish I'd never come –

PAULA. It's hardly ya worst mistake.

Beat.

BARBARA. I think ya've said enough.

PAULA. Listen –

LORETTA (*to* BARBARA). She didn't even want us here. (*To* PAULA.) What a nasty piece of fuckin' work you are –

PAULA. Mam –

LORETTA. Abigail's close to tears over there –

Ya've crippled ya mother –

PAULA. It's only a dress –

LORETTA. Ya fuckin' poisonous –

PAULA. Mam?

Beat.

BARBARA. It's not just a dress.

LORETTA. You heard her –

LORETTA *grabs* PAULA*'s things, forces them into her suitcase, punches in anything she can get her hands on, the Pomagne bottle, the Cock Straws, the broken Casio, as:*

Ya've made it perfectly clear nothin's good enough for ya, that ya can't bear us, so why don't ya just get out –

LORETTA *thrusts* PAULA*'s suitcase at her.*

PAULA. Mam?

Silence.

Abigail?

LORETTA *drags* ABIGAIL *away from* PAULA.

LORETTA. Leave her –

ABIGAIL *shakes her head but* LORETTA *grabs it, holds it still.*

PAULA. It's you I feel sorry for, Loretta –

LORETTA. Aye, fuck the lot of us, if ya goin', go –

LORETTA *forces* PAULA *out the door, slams it.*

Silence.

BARBARA *picks up the wedding dress, clings to it.*

Howay, Mam, ya gonna ruin the night, away and wash ya face, we've to go any minute.

(*To* JOLENE.) You, stick ya head round the door, and see if Marvin and Max are still with us.

JOLENE *nips outside, nips back.*

JOLENE. They look like they're outside of Buckingham Palace.

LORETTA. Whack a bit of lippy on then, ya'll look like the odd one out.

JOLENE. Really?

LORETTA. Quickly.

JOLENE *beelines for the mirror, revels in applying lipstick.*

Come on, Mam, get up, ya're alright –

LORETTA *helps* BARBARA *up, directs her to and into the bathroom.*

(*To* JOLENE.) Can ya take that outside, please, and tell the lads we'll not be a tick.

JOLENE. No bother.

Exit JOLENE.

LORETTA *takes a condom from her make-up bag and one of the Cock Straws, opens it and demonstrates how to apply it to the male member for* ABIGAIL.

LORETTA. This'll, fingers crossed, be much bigger in real life but ya get the general gist.

Ya nip the end, so's it doesn't explode, pop it on the top like a Wee Willie Winkie hat and roll the sides down, right the way down to his knackers, alright?

Make sure it goes all the way down or it'll fly off and have
ya eye out, okay?

ABIGAIL *nods.*

Here –

LORETTA *puts the finishing touches to* ABIGAIL*'s hair, as:*

ABIGAIL. Mam?

LORETTA. Yes, love?

ABIGAIL. Do ya think we could make it to The Camp Champ's
Championship at some point?

LORETTA. Listen –

Ya've got lipstick teeth, do this –

LORETTA *rubs her front teeth with her finger and*
ABIGAIL *copies.*

And, if anyone asks, you're eighteen, I'm twenty-one and
we're sisters, alright?

ABIGAIL *nods.*

Come on, then –

LORETTA *grabs* ABIGAIL*'s hand and they exit as the*
bathroom door opens to reveal BARBARA*, twenty-one, in*
her wedding dress, her face thick with cream, leading us into
the next scene.

Scene Three

1961.

Saturday 22nd July. BARBARA*'s wedding day.*

BARBARA, *twenty-one, is downstage centre in her wedding dress, her face thick with cream.*

At the mirror stands SYLVIA, *twenty, her hair in rollers, back to* BARBARA, *as:*

SYLVIA. Have ya heard off him?

BARBARA. He's gone.

    SYLVIA *looks to* BARBARA, *looks back to the mirror.*

SYLVIA. There's this girl I know, knows a doctor that does it for seventy pound.

    Comes straight to ya house, no questions asked.

    Ya can use mine if ya don't want him at yours, if ya worried about folk seein'. Our mam, she works all hours these days –

    Enter EDITH, *forty, from the bathroom with a fistful of tissue.*

EDITH (*to* BARBARA). How's that?

BARBARA. It stings.

EDITH. It's lead-based, but diarrhoea'll be out ya system in a week, weddin' pictures are for life.

SYLVIA. Ya look like Connie Francis –

EDITH. Does she toffee, leave her be –

    EDITH *hands* BARBARA *the tissue.*

    Get it off.

    EDITH *sparks up a Woodbine, smokes, helps herself to a small sherry as* BARBARA *wipes the cream from her face.*

I said we'd meet the photographer in the Goon Bar for
prenuptial snaps –

BARBARA. I'm nervous.

EDITH. Ya'll not be by noon, with a cup of tea and a boiled egg
under your belt, it'll be think on and look sharp, that's all
ya'll need concern yaself with today, that and the husband,
that and Neil.

BARBARA. There still seems so much to do –

EDITH. I've had more complicated baths.

Beat.

SYLVIA. I'll probably cry, I always cry at weddins –

BARBARA. Me, too –

EDITH. A weddin's no place for emotions, Barbara.

SYLVIA. My mam says that, too, about weddins, Mrs
Richardson, about emotions, there's some that faint, isn't
there –

EDITH. That's sinners for ya, Sylvia, weighed down with guilt,
their conscience pushin' them to the depths, to the Devil.

SYLVIA. My dad says she doesn't deserve to laugh or cry if
she's gonna be such a miserable witch about it –

But I agree with you, Mrs Richardson, a weddin's the last
place for emotions –

EDITH. What does he do again, ya father?

SYLVIA. He's a nightwatchman.

BARBARA. Works all hours, doesn't he, Sylvia?

EDITH. As many hours as Neil up that Rowntree's factory?

SYLVIA. Probably not.

EDITH. Probably not, no.

Beat.

SYLVIA. Neil's lovely, isn't he, Mrs Richardson?

EDITH. Ya'd struggle to find a finer gentleman this side of Carlisle, and such an upstandin' member of the community. (*To* SYLVIA.) Ya know he's on first-name terms with the cousin of the Mayor of Sunderland.

SYLVIA. He never is – (*To* BARBARA.) Ya never said.

EDITH. I forget her name, but he did tell uz, what was it again, Barbara?

BARBARA. Gloria.

SYLVIA. Oh, to be called Gloria, Mrs Richardson, can you imagine?

EDITH. It's another world, isn't it?

SYLVIA. I still can't believe he's sat and had his tea with the Mayor, can you, Barbara?

BARBARA. No.

SYLVIA. Did he say what they had?

BARBARA. I don't know –

SYLVIA. I imagine it was somethin' posh, all twenty-five courses of it, what do they even eat, the posh?

BARBARA (*snaps*). I wouldn't know –

SYLVIA (*snaps*). I only asked.

EDITH *stubs out her cigarette.*

EDITH. Ya'll find out soon enough, though, won't ya, Barbara?

Silence.

(*To* SYLVIA.) Bring her clips, the paisley bag by the bath.

SYLVIA. Yes, Mrs Richardson.

Exit SYLVIA.

EDITH. Ya wanna calm yaself down, lady, ya hear?

BARBARA *nods.*

The lass was only makin' conversation, she's tryin', we all are –

It's nerves, they'll pass –

Up –

EDITH *drags* BARBARA *up so she's standing in front of her, picks at and tends to her wedding dress over the next section.*

If we get the weather, no one'll cotton on this isn't pure white.

BARBARA. It's nice –

EDITH. It's cream, it's coarse.

BARBARA. No one cares –

EDITH (*snaps*). I bloody care.

SYLVIA (*off, shouts*). The sandy-coloured seashell bag, Mrs Richardson?

EDITH (*shouts*). Paisley, Sylvia.

EDITH *picks up the veil, brushes it down, positions it in place.*

What an awful, painful day.

Enter SYLVIA. *She hands hairclips to* EDITH, *who pins* BARBARA*'s veil firmly in place over the next section.*

SYLVIA. What was Barbara's birth like, Mrs Richardson?

EDITH. Nothing to do with you, young lady.

I fell on bonfire night, had you in the summer and by Christmas 1940 he was gone.

Knew in my heart of hearts he'd never really wanted uz but it was a time of rationin', ya'd to take what ya could.

Turned out love had gone to war with him.

Get gone.

(*To* SYLVIA.) You –

Over the next section, SYLVIA *takes a seat,* EDITH *stands behind her and removes her rollers, as:*

SYLVIA. I couldn't live without my home comforts, Mrs Richardson.

EDITH. If ya'd no choice, ya could.

SYLVIA. My Reg for one'd sooner mangle his own wet washin' than tackle a day's hard graft on nowt but a thimbleful of powdered egg and a black bullet.

EDITH. It's a surprise any of us went full term –

BARBARA. What was my birth like?

EDITH. The Somme.

Beat.

BARBARA. Was my dad there?

EDITH. What do you think?

Neil will be, though, cigar in hand, pressed shirt, copper-clipped braces and enough heart to teach it right from wrong.

He's a good man.

Beat.

SYLVIA. Am I done?

EDITH. Get gone.

SYLVIA *makes for the mirror, twirls.*

SYLVIA. Gina Lollobrigida eat ya heart out.

BARBARA. Ya look beautiful.

EDITH. It's gonna be a beautiful day.

SYLVIA. I know it is, Mrs Richardson.

EDITH. Then a smile or two'd not go amiss.

BARBARA *attempts a smile.*

(*Snaps.*) Less gums.

BARBARA. Sorry.

EDITH. It won't be lavish but it'll be lovely and I imagine Neil scrubs up a treat.

SYLVIA. Rock Hudson.

EDITH. There ya go, there's matinee-idol looks there for starters.

What were his family like when we went round, Barbara, tell Sylvia.

Silence.

They'd a lovely home, Sylvia, a bright-white house, eat dinner not tea, have a lavatory instead of a toilet.

He wears spectacles, she a brooch.

They say, 'pardon', don't they, Barbara, say, 'pardon'? Instead of 'what?' Tell Sylvia.

BARBARA. They say 'pardon'.

EDITH. When they opened their front door, the mam and the dad, Annie and Edward, they said, 'How do you do?' To me. How do I do?

Some women long their whole lives to be asked that, to be asked how they are, if just by a complete stranger.

It was his parents that organised it so we could actually have the vows on camp, up the chapel, it's not the norm. They understand, though, the importance of things, he's their only son, the apple of Annie's eye, wait till ya see her opulent array of outfits, Sylvia –

(*To* SYLVIA.) It means 'fancy'.

SYLVIA (*to herself, slowly*). Op-u-lent. (*Quickly.*) Opulent, opulent –

EDITH. And to raise management with a capital M, that's parentin', that's due care and attention right there. My mother'd sooner Brasso the baptismal font than hold her kids –

Get this right and ya're flyin', there's many a lass'd swap places with you right now, many. Isn't that right, Sylvia?

SYLVIA. That's right, Mrs Richardson.

EDITH. Ya can be good again, Barbara, redeemed, a lifetime away from what's stood in front of uz –

Mary Magdalene in off-white.

I don't even like seein' ya in that dress, it breaks my heart.

BARBARA. Cos ya losin' uz?

EDITH. Cos ya too bloody fat for it.

Beat.

BARBARA. I'm not fat –

EDITH. Ya're pushin' it out, I'm not stupid –

BARBARA. I'm not –

EDITH. Ya'll make a song and dance about owt –

BARBARA. It's this dress –

EDITH. I'm not stupid –

EDITH *pushes* BARBARA*'s stomach in, is forceful,* BARBARA *pulls away.*

BARBARA. Careful –

EDITH (*snaps*). I can see ya deliberately doin' it, Barbara –

EDITH *goes for* BARBARA *again.*

SYLVIA. Mrs Richardson –

SYLVIA *steps in, doesn't mean to but grabs* EDITH*'s arm.*

EDITH *pushes* SYLVIA *away.*

EDITH (*to* SYLVIA). See if ya mother doesn't hear about this.

SYLVIA *is stunned, looks like she might cry.*

Away and wash ya face.

Exit SYLVIA.

Remember ya place, Barbara, today has nothin' to do with you thanks to you.

EDITH *sits, sparks up a Woodbine, smokes, sips at a small sherry.*

BARBARA. You said contraception was evil.

EDITH *stands, livid.*

EDITH. I said intercourse was, too –

BARBARA. 'Honesty guides good people, dishonesty destroys treacherous people.'

EDITH. Don't dare preach at me –

BARBARA. I wasn't –

EDITH. Bringin' shame on the family, on me – (*Snaps.*) No.

Take it to ya rosary and beg Mary Mother for strength and for guidance –

BARBARA. I'm sorry.

EDITH (*snaps*). I said, beg –

BARBARA *takes out her rosary beads, sits, closes her eyes, prays with them over the next section.*

EDITH *sits, pins her hat in place.*

Enter SYLVIA, *fussing with her hair in the mirror, as:*

Ya know nothin' about love, about bein' a mother, about anythin', the pair of ya.

They say ya can't call yaself a woman until ya've been a mother.

SYLVIA. Who says?

EDITH (*snaps*). Everyone says.

EDITH *snatches the rosary beads from* BARBARA.

Stop that now and stand up straight, let uz look at ya –

EDITH *drags* BARBARA *up so she's standing in front of her.*

Awful cheeks, you're ya nana facially –

BARBARA *shifts on her feet, only slightly but it draws* EDITH*'s attention to her stomach.*

(*Snaps.*) I told ya to stop that –

EDITH *pushes* BARBARA*'s stomach in, more forceful than before. It hurts,* BARBARA *pulls away.*

BARBARA. Ya'll hurt it.

EDITH. Do ya think Neil'll want to see it?

BARBARA. No –

EDITH. Then put it away.

BARBARA. He has to see it eventually –

EDITH. And when he does he'll be proud as punch, cos it'll be his then, we can celebrate then.

BARBARA. But it's not his –

EDITH. And what a shame that is, what a shame you are, Barbara.

To think of ya with that boy. It's disgustin'.

Beat.

BARBARA. His name's Teddy –

EDITH. Don't dare say that name today.

BARBARA. I thought he might come –

EDITH. He doesn't want ya and you want nowt with him.

The second you get home, ya to steer well clear of that Empire Palace Theatre.

BARBARA. I will.

EDITH. If anyone asks ya to go, ya say no, ya make ya excuses.

BARBARA. Have ya seen him play?

EDITH. Ya say no –

BARBARA. They come for miles around to hear him on that piano –

EDITH. You dare go there to see that boy –

BARBARA (*snaps*). His name's Teddy.

EDITH (*shouts*). I won't tell you again.

BARBARA (*screams*). I don't want to marry Neil –

EDITH (*shouts*). Ya have to marry someone, Barbara.

> EDITH *stubs out her cigarette.*
>
> *Beat.*

BARBARA. There's this girl Sylvia knows, knows a doctor –

EDITH. Go into the bathroom, please, Sylvia.

> SYLVIA *looks at* BARBARA, *looks at* EDITH.

SYLVIA. Mrs Richardson?

EDITH (*snaps*). I won't tell ya again.

> SYLVIA *makes for the bathroom.*
>
> *She goes in but doesn't close the door, watches what follows, as:*
>
> EDITH *takes* BARBARA's *hands in hers, her grip too tight.*

Our Father, who art in Heaven,
Hallowed be Thy name –

SYLVIA. Ya're hurtin' her –

EDITH (*to* SYLVIA). Close that door –

Thy kingdom come,
Thy will be done –

BARBARA. I can't –

EDITH. On Earth as it is in Heaven –

BARBARA. Stop it –

EDITH. Give us this day our daily bread –

SYLVIA. Mrs Richardson, please –

EDITH. And forgive us our trespasses –

BARBARA. Please?

EDITH. You're a sinner.

SYLVIA. She didn't sin –

EDITH (*shouts*, *to* SYLVIA). Close it, Sylvia –

BARBARA (*screams*). I've done nothin' wrong –

EDITH (*screams*). Hate the sin but love the sinner –

EDITH *slaps* BARBARA, *catches her breath, as:*

You'll marry him, Barbara, and there'll not be another word said on the matter, on him, that bastard, ya hear?

I never loved ya father but he never loved me. Neil, he worships the bones of ya, he'll give ya everythin'. He's a world without cobbles and chimneys, women and washin', miners, grime.

He lives in a world of colour and you don't know how lucky you are.

At your age, younger than you, I was at war, we all were. With the world. With each other. Ourselves.

Silence.

BARBARA. I want to call her Paula.

If it's a girl –

EDITH. Ya'll name her after ya Nana Loretta, she's tantamount to a Saint in the church's eyes.

BARBARA. But I like Paula –

EDITH. That woman single-handedly raised forty pounds for the Spastic Society by bakin' nowt but Swiss rolls and she doesn't even like jam –

BARBARA. I didn't want this life –

EDITH. It's too late to take it back –

BARBARA (*snaps*). I don't love him –

EDITH (*snaps*). This isn't about love.

EDITH *sits, sparks up a Woodbine, smokes. She breaks down.*

SYLVIA. Mrs Richardson?

EDITH (*snaps*). Leave uz –

She composes herself.

We held this country together, women, daft bits of lasses with the secret strength of ten men in each of us.

And you, look at ya, not a hint of gratitude, not nowt.

Ya wanna look out there, folk lappin' about in the pool, holdin' hands, not a care in this world, just row upon row of chalet lines, little boxes full up with little lives, little bits of love.

There's nowt most folk wouldn't do for that life, nowt I wouldn't.

And I'm glad for ya, elated for ya, look at uz, look how happy I am, ya're set for life and what have I got? For all my work, for my strugglin' and battlin', for my war? (*Screams.*) What?

For believin' in one true, one divine God?

I've nothin'.

Beat.

BARBARA. It's not too late for ya to start again.

EDITH *stubs out her cigarette, necks her sherry, stands, fixes her face.*

EDITH. Men are all the same, Barbara, they let women down.

If ya want my advice, ya'll hold ya breath and hope for the best –

A knock at the door.

That'll be ya Auntie Fran with the flowers. I'll give ya a
minute, tend to ya face, compose yaself.

What an awful, painful day –

Exit EDITH.

SYLVIA *walks over to* BARBARA, *takes her hand, holds
her, kisses her lips, there is a moment between the two,
intimate but not sexual.*

BARBARA *breaks down.*

SYLVIA *slowly undresses* BARBARA, *as:*

BARBARA. I used to want to be a secretary, learn shorthand,
go to a cocktail party, breathe.

I used to want to be a woman before I was a mother.

I'm not ready to go yet –

SYLVIA *folds the wedding dress, hands it to* BARBARA.

She drafted the redcoats in to usher in their smart red blazers.

We waited forty-five minutes for the reception cos no one'd
cancelled Cumbrian Wrestlin'.

I come away with a fish kettle.

I come away with rice in my hair.

I come away with a bruise on the top of my arm from where
he grabbed uz to first-kiss uz.

To honour and to obey.

During sickness and during health.

Enter LORETTA, *forty-eight,* JOLENE, *twenty-eight, and*
ABIGAIL, *thirty.*

Lighting change, as:

We came back to the same chalet every year, the same
wardrobe, mattress, faces.

Everyone knew Loretta by name, doted on her, the little girl who asked questions, always asked why?

Why do birds fly? Why do ladies kiss gentlemen? Why are ya cryin'?

I couldn't stop not lovin' her.

And I could never answer her questions cos I didn't know why, I didn't care why.

Exit SYLVIA.

They put wallpaper over wallpaper here.

They put paint on paint.

While we put mascara on mascara, lipstick on lipstick, hairspray to hold everythin' together.

Cos it was once glorious here, we were once colour.

We ballroom danced, made friends we thought we'd keep for ever, conceived Paula.

I've never seen a little girl so happy as I did with her here.

Bonniest Baby 1969, proud as punch.

My bonny baby, the other mothers clammin' for a hold but I never let her go, not once.

And I miss that.

Her happy.

Me here with her.

The pair of us back behind these four walls where we once had the chance to be any single thing in this world that we wanted.

BARBARA *hands the dress to* LORETTA.

LORETTA *hands the dress to* ABIGAIL.

ABIGAIL *destroys the dress, lays it out over the bedside table like a tablecloth, leading us into the next scene.*

Scene Four

2010.

Thursday 22nd July. BARBARA*'s seventieth birthday.*

BARBARA*, seventy,* LORETTA*, forty-eight,* JOLENE*, twenty-eight and* ABIGAIL*, thirty, are sat around the small bedside table on mismatching chairs in the chalet centre. They have wine but no food, there's balloons, banners and a cake box.*

JOLENE *is lost in her heart-throb scrapbook, a cut-and-paste mess of dream cars, dream dresses and dream decor. She holds it up, a picture of a kitchen.*

JOLENE. This is our kitchen.

LORETTA. It's bloody lovely.

JOLENE. I knew all the things I'd've made for him in it, cooked them, cared for him –

    JOLENE *turns the page on her heart-throb scrapbook, a picture of a sofa.*

    This is Linda Barker, it looks green in the picture but it's pistachio, his favourite colour –

    JOLENE *turns the page on her heart-throb scrapbook, a picture of the von Trapp family from* The Sound of Music.

    I wanted kids –

LORETTA. Course.

    JOLENE *turns the page on her heart-throb scrapbook, a picture of an idyllic wedding scene.*

JOLENE. This is how I saw our weddin'.

LORETTA. Ya nana's tryin' to be seventy here –

JOLENE. I even knew the font I wanted for the invites.

LORETTA (*snaps*). We know –

JOLENE (*snaps*). I'd planned everythin' to the letter –

JOLENE *turns the page on her heart-throb scrapbook, a picture of Flamingo Land.*

Where we'd go on day trips –

JOLENE *turns the page on her heart-throb scrapbook, a picture of a beef Wellington.*

What we'd make at dinner parties –

JOLENE *turns the page on her heart-throb scrapbook, a picture of Danny and Sandy from* Grease.

What we'd wear for fancy dress –

BARBARA (*snaps*). He's not comin' –

JOLENE (*snaps*). Alright –

LORETTA (*snaps*). Don't snap at ya nana like that.

JOLENE *clings to the scrapbook for her dear life, sobs.*

Silence.

What are we gonna do with you?

JOLENE *shakes her head.*

Beat.

What's he said?

JOLENE. That he can't love uz –

LORETTA. What's not to love?

JOLENE. That it's impossible.

That I'm clingy and intense and, more than likely, need him more than he needs me –

LORETTA. Then why propose?

JOLENE. He said it's part and parcel of his job, that and the fact that he falls in and out of love really quickly.

The funny thing is, that's what I loved best about him, how quick he knew how nice I was.

LORETTA. When's he said this?

JOLENE. He's text uz.

LORETTA. And who is he to go round makin' and breakin' hearts?

JOLENE. He's absolutely gorgeous, Mam.

LORETTA. Then, tell him 'no', say ya'll not take that for an answer, ya wanna see him, tell him straight –

JOLENE (*snaps*). It's over, Mam, alright?

LORETTA (*snaps*). I'm only tryin' to help.

Beat.

JOLENE. I'm maybes just one of them lasses that's destined never to get married –

LORETTA. Of course ya not one of them lasses –

JOLENE. They're not all ugly as sin, some of them look like me –

LORETTA. You're marriage material if ever a lass was, ya need to sit down, take stock and really think this through –

JOLENE. I've thought it through –

JOLENE *slams her heart-throb scrapbook to the floor, kicks it across the chalet floor.*

I've an airin' cupboard full of pregnancy tests from eBay for when the time was right, thought I knew exactly what time everythin' was gonna be right, planned every last detail to my specifications, to his specifications, whoever he is –

LORETTA. There's no point windin' yaself up about it –

JOLENE. I'm past carin' –

LORETTA. Ya do nowt but care, that's your trouble –

JOLENE. I've got somethin' to tell ya, Mam.

   I'm never gettin' married.

LORETTA. Look at uz –

JOLENE. My mind's made up –

LORETTA. Ya listenin'?

   JOLENE nods.

   I've maybes not set the best example, but ya dad, look at
   him, as much use as a bloody Christmas card, but he's there,
   he's mine and I know I hate him as much as I love him but I
   wouldn't, I couldn't swap him for the world –

   I know ya can't always see it but there is love there, there's a
   million magical bits of it –

JOLENE. Where?

LORETTA (*snaps*). Everywhere.

   Cos I know we argue like cat and dog but that's worth the
   battlin', the scars, the umpteen years of heartache and
   loneliness –

JOLENE. Is it?

LORETTA. Cos, like Cheryl Cole says, ya've gotta fight fight
   fight fight fight for love, Jolene.

JOLENE. It shouldn't be that much effort, surely?

LORETTA. What?

JOLENE. Just lovin' someone.

LORETTA. What me and your dad've got runs deeper than
   love.

   He's the one thing that makes uz so happy I wanna fuckin'
   explode –

   ABIGAIL *starts to laugh.*

   Beat.

   What?

ABIGAIL. Sorry –

ABIGAIL laughs harder, louder.

LORETTA joins her, thinks she's made some shit-hot joke, she nudges JOLENE to join in, they all piss themselves, exchanging glances, as:

LORETTA. What's so funny?

ABIGAIL. You –

LORETTA. Was it what I said about explodin'?

ABIGAIL shakes her head, can't speak.

It was, wasn't it?

They all have one last blast of laughter, calm down, wipe their comedy tears away.

I don't even know I'm doin' it half the time, me and your Charlie'll laugh like drains for hours over nowt –

What was it I said?

ABIGAIL. Ya're just, God –

You actually believe that, don't ya?

Beat.

LORETTA. Believe what?

ABIGAIL. That you and Dad're somethin' special –

LORETTA. We are.

ABIGAIL. That ya actually make each other happy –

LORETTA. We've been married thirty year –

ABIGAIL. Ya can't stand him.

LORETTA. I love the bones of that man.

JOLENE. I've never seen ya smile –

LORETTA. I can't smile wide enough.

JOLENE. I wish that was true.

LORETTA. It's you I'm tryin' to help.

ABIGAIL. By makin' out she's nowt without a lad –

LORETTA. It's her that's desperate, not me –

JOLENE. I'm not desperate –

LORETTA. Ya've a fuckin' book on it, get it, I'll show ya –

JOLENE. I've seen it.

LORETTA. It says all ya ever need is to be married.

JOLENE. I wonder where I get that from?

LORETTA. From ya magazines, Jolene.

ABIGAIL. Ya tell her she's nowt without a husband –

LORETTA. She cannet very well marry herself –

JOLENE. I'm not gettin' married –

LORETTA. Since all of five minutes ago?

ABIGAIL. That she's not pretty without one –

LORETTA. Since ya realised there's no one out there wants ya –

ABIGAIL. That's not true –

LORETTA. And decided to take it out on me?

JOLENE. I'm not –

LORETTA (*snaps*). Well, no.

    Me and ya dad're content.

    We laugh, we have food fights, he's never cheated on uz –

JOLENE. I never said he did –

LORETTA (*snaps*). He wouldn't.

    (*To* JOLENE.) Ya know ya sister's only stickin' up for ya cos
    she's jealous.

JOLENE. Of what?

LORETTA. Look at ya, Jolene, ya gorgeous –

ABIGAIL. If anyone envies her, it's you –

LORETTA. As long as she's married, she's the pretty one, well, I know better –

ABIGAIL. And what do you know?

LORETTA. That it's not all sunshine and lollipops behind closed doors.

ABIGAIL. There's nothin' behind our door.

LORETTA. Exactly.

ABIGAIL. Ya'll say anythin', won't ya?

LORETTA. Jealous cos she got the hips as well as the happiness –

ABIGAIL (*snaps*). I am happy.

LORETTA (*snaps*). And what would you ever have to fuckin' smile about?

Beat.

ABIGAIL. It doesn't matter –

LORETTA. Exactly, nowt –

LORETTA *pours herself a drink, as:*

Ya dad'll go wild when I tell him the way ya spoke to uz, the pair of ya, see if I don't –

ABIGAIL. He'll not even be listenin' –

LORETTA (*screams*). One more word from you and I'll fling ya through that fuckin' window –

BARBARA. Did ya ask her and she said no?

LORETTA. Sorry?

BARBARA. Or did ya tell her not to come?

LORETTA *takes a drink.*

LORETTA. Ring the Kaleidoscope, Jolene, and see what's
    holdin' them up –

BARBARA. I need to know –

LORETTA. The number's in the side pocket of my bag –

BARBARA. Loretta?

LORETTA. Ya pissed, Mam –

BARBARA (*snaps*). Please –

LORETTA (*snaps*). I didn't invite her, I've told ya –

    There's nowt for her here.

    Silence.

    LORETTA *raises her glass.*

    Happy birthday.

    LORETTA *toasts alone, drinks.*

    Silence.

    LORETTA *fusses with glasses, bottles and decorations,
    busies herself with no real purpose, as:*

    It's meant to be gorgeous, the food from that Kaleidoscope, I
    saw a sticky toffee puddin' fly by when we were in.

    I got this new top, nippin' at uz under the arms, only cheap
    but make an effort, I thought, go all out, so I did. She said in
    the shop it was all the rage –

    Probably takes ya back to the war, does it, Mam, sittin' here?
    We could do a parlour game in a bit, if ya like? Sardines, is
    it? Somethin' fishy, I can't remember –

    We can make do, cos that's what we do, we make do, isn't it?
    We make jokes, make songs, make the bed, the tea, make it
    clean again, it all okay again.

    There's no colour anywhere any more.

    My stomach thinks my throat's been cut.

    It won't be lavish but it will be lovely –

BARBARA. It's barely even bearable, Loretta.

Beat.

LORETTA. I've brought the whole family together for ya –

BARBARA. Not quite –

LORETTA. I blew up fifty balloons.

BARBARA. That was Claude –

LORETTA. I baked a cake.

BARBARA. Ya bought it, ya told uz –

LORETTA. I bought a cake. Coconut. Ya favourite.

Beat.

BARBARA. Did ya tell her how important this was?

LORETTA. She wants nowt to do with me either, I'm hurtin' too –

BARBARA. At least you got to speak to her –

LORETTA. I've never spoke to her, I've not her number –

BARBARA. Ya wanna be ashamed.

LORETTA. I did it for you –

BARBARA. Gettin' my hopes up –

LORETTA. It's her loss –

BARBARA. It's my loss, she's my daughter.

Beat.

LORETTA. I'm ya daughter, too.

BARBARA. It's not the same.

LORETTA *pours herself a drink, as:*

LORETTA. I ordered Love Hearts with ya name on but they never come in time. Claude said I shouldn't've bothered, 'Ya could leap out a cake with ya tits ablaze and she'd still not bat an eye,' he said.

I was livid, didn't speak to him all the rest of that day.

She drinks.

Our clothes, they used to face each other in the wardrobe, they face opposite directions now. A big fat gap in the middle where we keep that blow-up bed we got from Tesco's for if we ever have guests, but no one ever comes.

No one new ever comes.

LORETTA *looks at* BARBARA, *a little girl lost, she breaks down.*

ABIGAIL *holds* LORETTA, *is tender, strokes her hair as she breaks her whole heart.*

Silence.

LORETTA *pushes* ABIGAIL *away.*

ABIGAIL. Mam?

LORETTA (*snaps*). I'm fuckin' champion –

LORETTA *composes herself, pours herself a drink, downs it.*

Still wearin' White Musk, I see.

ABIGAIL. Me?

LORETTA. It's all over uz.

I'll have to do my hair again now so thank you.

ABIGAIL. I was tryin' to help –

LORETTA. Well, ya've not helped, I fuckin' stink.

I'm surprised Charlie'll come anywhere near ya.

ABIGAIL. There's nothin' wrong with uz.

LORETTA. Where's ya outfit from, the joke shop?

ABIGAIL. Ya don't have to say them things.

LORETTA. You make uz say them.

ABIGAIL *smiles.*

What?

ABIGAIL. I used to listen to you.

LORETTA. Ya've never listened.

ABIGAIL. I used to think ya wanted the best for uz.

LORETTA. I've given ya everythin'.

ABIGAIL. I used to believe what ya said.

LORETTA. So?

ABIGAIL. I was sixteen.

Beat.

LORETTA. Wild horses wouldn't've held ya back, Abigail.

ABIGAIL. You should've held uz back.

Beat.

LORETTA. This is ya nana's night so maybes ya wanna stop makin' such a song and dance about things?

Ya normal now, aren't ya, ya settled now –

ABIGAIL. Me and Charlie sittin' in a tree?

LORETTA. That lad is one in a bloody million, remember that, remember no one else would've wanted ya, I'd've been stuck with ya for ever.

And I'm glad for ya, elated for ya, look at uz, look how happy I am that you, of all of us, have landed someone like him –

ABIGAIL. I'm leavin' Charlie.

LORETTA. To his own devices?

ABIGAIL. I don't love him.

LORETTA. Lasses like you don't leave lads like Charlie, that's the rosé talkin' – (*To* JOLENE.) She's pissed.

BARBARA. She's not even drinkin'.

ABIGAIL. I've never loved him.

LORETTA. I'm not bein' funny, but have I just walked into *The* fuckin' *Twilight Zone*?

JOLENE. Listen to her –

LORETTA. No, let uz get this straight. You are leavin' Charlie? Ya husband Charlie?

BARBARA. That's what she said –

LORETTA. My Charlie?

BARBARA. Loretta, sit down –

LORETTA. He's threw her out and she's tryin' to make out it's mutual.

She's been dumped.

And isn't that rich, you sat there dumped and ya dare to slag my marriage –

ABIGAIL. It was my decision.

JOLENE. See?

LORETTA. Give it a fortnight, ya'll be beggin' him to take ya back.

ABIGAIL. He's not a bad person –

LORETTA. Ten of you –

ABIGAIL. But I could never be truly happy with him, like ya meant to be, like ya sometimes, just sometimes see people bein' with each other –

Like that.

He didn't ever understand uz –

LORETTA. There's no one understands you, me included.

I wish I'd never introduced ya's, it's me that'll come out of this smellin' like shite –

ABIGAIL. I wish ya hadn't –

LORETTA. Well, I won't be takin' sides, I'll tell him every last word ya've said tonight, and that's less, much less than that lad deserves –

BARBARA. Can ya just, for five mintues, Loretta, let her speak –

LORETTA. He calls ya, ya know –

ABIGAIL. I don't care.

LORETTA. Says ya'll barely look at him, find the time of day for him, like him, love him –

ABIGAIL (*snaps*). Have him –

LORETTA (*snaps*). I've got ya dad.

ABIGAIL (*snaps*). That's never stopped ya before –

Cos bein' like this, decidin' this, is the first time I've felt real in years.

I feel 3D –

LORETTA. What were ya before, a fuckin' hologram?

ABIGAIL (*snaps*). I was nowt.

LORETTA (*snaps*). Ya were nowt then and ya nowt now.

ABIGAIL *pulls out her suitcase, pops on her coat, buttons up, as:*

Ya not goin' now –

ABIGAIL. Have a lovely evenin', Nana –

LORETTA. Another drink, Mam?

ABIGAIL *kisses* BARBARA.

I'll open that other bottle of cava.

ABIGAIL (*to* BARBARA). Bye.

LORETTA (*to* ABIGAIL). Ya'll sit and have a glass, won't ya?

LORETTA *opens a bottle of cava, proceeds to pour drinks over the next section, as:*

If not for me, then for ya nana –

BARBARA. Let her go –

LORETTA. We should be celebratin' –

BARBARA. There's nowt to celebrate –

ABIGAIL *kisses* JOLENE.

LORETTA. Ya surely not this selfish, Abigail.

ABIGAIL (*to* JOLENE). Bye.

LORETTA (*snaps*). I raised ya better than this.

Beat.

ABIGAIL. See ya, Mam.

ABIGAIL *kisses* LORETTA, *makes for the door, as:*

LORETTA. Ya've spoilt it, ya know, ya nana's day, not your day – (*Snaps.*) Never yours –

ABIGAIL *tries the door, can't make it work.*

LORETTA *goes to her, grabs her suitcase from her, as:*

Cos it's gonna be the best night, I can feel it in my fanny –

LORETTA *proceeds to open* ABIGAIL's *suitcase, pulls free her belongings, throws them around the chalet.* ABIGAIL *tries to stop her, as:*

I've worked too hard for too long now for anyone to ruin anythin' –

ABIGAIL. Please?

LORETTA. For you in particular to ruin it –

ABIGAIL. Stop it –

LORETTA. Cos we'll get to the good bit eventually, we've just got to be patient –

ABIGAIL (*snaps*). Put them back –

LORETTA (*snaps*). We've to bide our time –

ABIGAIL (*shouts*). Let uz go –

LORETTA (*shouts*). Cos all things come to those who wait and we've been sat here fuckin' years –

She stops, catches her breath, as:

Sit down, Abigail.

ABIGAIL. I have to go.

LORETTA (*snaps*). I said, sit –

LORETTA *grabs* ABIGAIL, *forces her into a chair at the table.*

(*To* ABIGAIL.) You there –

LORETTA *grabs* JOLENE, *forces her into a chair at the table.*

(*To* JOLENE.) You there –

LORETTA *grabs* BARBARA, *forces her into a chair at the table.*

(*To* BARBARA.) And you there –

Have a drink, it's a party –

LORETTA *pours out more drinks, the glasses overflow, she's breaking down.*

She toasts.

Cheers.

She drinks.

Haven't I made it lovely?

The food'll be here any minute.

Didn't I do everythin' I could?

Mam?

Silence.

It's beautiful.

LORETTA *grabs fistfuls of cake, slams them down in front of* BARBARA, JOLENE *and* ABIGAIL.

Cake?

Well, go on then –

JOLENE *goes to take a corner of cake.*

Wait –

JOLENE *freezes.*

We didn't sing.

LORETTA *snatches the cake back, tries to mould a cake shape from the mess of icing and sponge, can't make it work,* JOLENE *tries to help.*

(*Snaps.*) I can do it –

LORETTA *stands, wipes her hands up the side of her top, holds her arms out to* BARBARA, *as if to dedicate her song, falls apart, as:*

(*Sings.*)
    Happy birthday to you,
    Happy birthday to you,
    Happy birthday, dear Mam,
    Happy birthday to you –

She breaks down.

Silence.

BARBARA *stands, walks over to a balloon, pops it, pops another and another, attacks them, pops them all, as:*

JOLENE *grabs her heart-throb scrapbook, rips a page from it, rips another and another, destroys it, as:*

LORETTA *takes in the carnage, downs the bottle of cava, kicks the cake box around the room and lets off a series of party poppers, as:*

ABIGAIL *takes a pack of Juicy Fruit from her suitcase.*

At the dressing table, she unwraps single sticks, lays them along its edge to resemble piano keys. She stretches her fingers, puts them to the 'piano' as the sound of a real piano, the grandest of them all, fills the whole chalet.

Everyone stops, listens.

She smiles.

She sings and plays 'Don't Let the Sun Go Down on Me' by Elton John.

She lets herself go completely and we see her for the first time.

The lights snap to black.

End.

A Nick Hern Book

Chalet Lines first published in Great Britain as a paperback original in 2012 by Nick Hern Books Limited, 14 Larden Road, London W3 7ST, in association with the Bush Theatre, London

Chalet Lines copyright © 2012 Lee Mattinson

Lee Mattinson has asserted his right to be identified as the author of this work

Cover image by Analogue
Cover design by Ned Hoste, 2H

Typeset by Nick Hern Books, London
Printed in Great Britain by Mimeo Ltd, Huntingdon, Cambridgeshire PE29 6XX

A CIP catalogue record for this book is available from the British Library

ISBN   978 1 84842 267 4